Working in Accountancy 2013

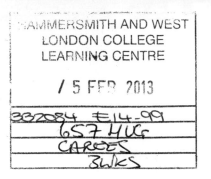
Working in Accountancy: A guide to qualifying and starting a successful career in accountancy

This second edition published in 2012 by Trotman Publishing, a division of Crimson Publishing Ltd, Westminster House, Kew Road, Richmond, Surrey TW9 2ND.

First edition published in 2011 by Trotman Publishing.

First edition written by Sherridan Hughes.
This second edition completely revised and updated by Natalie Sermon.

British Library Cataloguing in Publication Data
A catalogue record for this book is available from the British Library.

ISBN 978 1 84455 517 8

Typeset by IDSUK (DataConnection) Ltd
Printed and bound in the UK by Ashford Colour Press, Gosport, Hants

Working in Accountancy

A guide to qualifying and starting a successful career in accountancy

Sherridan Hughes and Natalie Sermon

Contents

Contents

Accounting Work Experience

AAT & SAGE TRAININGS WITH WORK EXPERIENCE

Get a head start on your accounting career by attending a work placement with a firm of Chartered Certified Accountants. We offer **Sage, AAT and other trainings with practical work experience placements.**

Discounts available for Level 2 & 3 AAT Qualification: Qualify in 10 weeks!

We offer the following courses:

- AAT
- Sage 50 Accounts Training
- Sage 50 Payroll
- Value Added Tax (VAT)
- Management Accounts
- Excel Spreadsheet
- Computer Based Assessments- AAT, ACCA, CIMA
- City and Guilds Bookkeeping & Accounts
- City and Guilds Computerised Accounts

The Training Place
of Excellence
where quality trainings & practical work placements take place

For more information

Visit www.thetrainingplace.org to download an application form, or you can contact us via:

Email: admin@thetrainingplace.org
Phone: 02072529331

Useful accounting terms

Y ou may be familiar with a few of these abbreviations already, or they might be completely new to you. This book usually expands these initialisations and other abbreviations and gives the terms in full the first time they appear; however, you can always turn back to this page to refresh your memory.

AAT: Association of Accounting Technicians

ACA: Designation of a qualified member of ICAEW or ICAI

ACCA: Association of Chartered Certified Accountants, or designation of a member thereof

ACMA: Associate Chartered Management Accountant – designation of a qualified member of CIMA

AIA: Association of International Accountants

ATT: Association of Taxation Technicians

Big Four: The four largest accountancy and professional services firms: Deloitte, KPMG, PwC and Ernst & Young

blue chip: Nationally recognised, well-established, high-quality, financially secure and stable firm, able to maintain performance in all economic climates

BTEC HND: Higher National Diploma awarded by the Business and Technology Education Council

CA: Designation of a qualified member of ICAS

CAI: Chartered Accountants Ireland

CAT: Certified accounting technician

Useful accounting terms

CEO: Chief executive officer

CFO: Chief financial officer

CIMA: Chartered Institute of Management Accountants

CIOT: Chartered Institute of Taxation

CIPFA: Chartered Institute of Public Finance and Accountancy

CIPP: Chartered Institute of Payroll Professionals

CPD: Continuing professional development

CSR: Corporate social responsibility

CTA: Chartered tax adviser

EU: European Union

FMCG: Fast-moving consumer goods

FSA: Financial Services Authority

FSP: Financial Skills Partnership

FTSE 100: The hundred largest UK companies listed on the London Stock Exchange and in *Financial Times* indices

FTSE 250: The 250 largest UK companies listed on the London Stock Exchange and in *Financial Times* indices

GAAP: Generally accepted accounting principles

GAAS: Generally accepted auditing standards

HMRC: Her Majesty's Revenue & Customs

HR: Human resources

ICAEW: Institute of Chartered Accountants in England and Wales

ICAS: Institute of Chartered Accountants of Scotland

IFA: Institute of Financial Accountants

IFRS: International Financial Reporting Standards

IPD: Initial professional development

IPDS: Initial Professional Development Scheme

NAO: National Audit Office

NGO: Non-governmental organisation

NVQ: National Vocational Qualification

PER: Practical Experience Requirement

POB: Professional Oversight Board

PwC: PricewaterhouseCoopers

SMEs: Small and medium-sized enterprises

UCAS: Universities and Colleges Admissions Service

Introduction

The common stereotype of the boring, serious accountant, tapping away on a calculator and poring over spreadsheets in the backroom, is often far from the reality. Yes, at the beginning of your career there may be some routine number-crunching, but how much depends on the sector, specialism and role in which you find yourself. Accountancy is actually a varied, influential, prestigious and lucrative profession. It is viewed as an excellent springboard into senior decision-making roles, which is clear from the fierce competition for training places. It also involves a great deal more contact with people than you might expect – which is one of the reasons why team-working and interpersonal skills are emphasised by employers.

You will find an accountant in nearly every business in the UK. There may even be more professionally qualified accountants in the UK than in the rest of the European Union (EU) countries put together. The Financial Reporting Council's Professional Oversight Board's (POB's) publication *Key Facts and Trends in the Accountancy Profession* (June 2012) stated that, in the UK and the Republic of Ireland, the seven main accountancy bodies currently support, qualify and represent more than 312,000 members and in excess of 170,000 students.

Accountants can be found in all sectors, ranging from the most obvious financial services and commerce to manufacturing and the not-for-profit sector. The roles can vary too, and can include highly technical and analytical work, the production of financial reports, financial control and strategic planning and management. Roles can be internal, within an organisation, or external, within professional and advisory services. Accountancy can provide a solid foundation for broader commercial, operational and systems roles as well. A large proportion of board members are qualified in accountancy and it is clearly a qualification that exhibits credibility and marketability, and can boost career prospects. Indeed, a sound understanding of finance is often viewed as imperative for a director.

You don't have to worry about the degree subject you have studied: accountancy is open to graduates of any discipline. However, be warned: the selection criteria and professional qualifications are rigorous. You will need to ensure that you are thoroughly prepared, with a strong academic record, impressive CV and good understanding of the various qualifications, roles and specialisms involved in the profession. Of course, you do not have to be a graduate, and there are school-leaver and on-the-job programmes that can lead to a professional qualification as well.

If you are thinking about and researching accountancy as a possible career path, this book aims to provide all the information you need to make well-informed decisions. This includes choosing between the main professional bodies and the qualifications they offer, the associated costs and the careers to which they may lead. The accountancy profession is a highly competitive arena, so the book provides help in finding training places and gives tips to ensure that you make a strong application. Jobs in accountancy are highly competitive – in 2011 Grant Thornton (an organisation dealing with independent assurance, tax and advisory firms) had 8,500 applications for only 230 trainee places. Alternative entry points and routes for those without the required UCAS points, or perhaps with minimal educational qualifications, will also be discussed.

So why is accountancy so popular and why do so many people choose the profession? What exactly is attracting them?

A survey of graduates for 2012 identified the aspects of the profession that influenced people to enter it (see Table 1).

TABLE 1: Why do people work in accountancy?

Reason for entering profession	Percentage of graduates
Good long-term career prospects	80%
Opportunity to gain professional qualifications	67%
Good job security	57%
Availability of jobs	55%
Quality of training and development	54%
Starting salaries	52%
Prestige of the job	50%
Interesting content of the work	46%
Able to use your degree subject	46%

Source: The UK Graduate Careers Survey 2012 (High Fliers Research Limited)/*The Times*

Coming out top of the reasons to apply to accountancy is that it has 'good long-term career prospects'. It seems to be important and valued in the current economic climate. The opportunity to gain a professional qualification is still important, with people recognising that professional development is a safe ticket to a stable and successful career. It is noteworthy that only 46% of respondents mentioned finding the subject interesting; this may change when they are working in the field, but it is not what attracted them to the profession in the first place. High starting salaries and security, which have a difference of only five percentage points between them, will no doubt be an even greater attraction in the future, given the increasing cost of higher education.

People who are good with numbers often gravitate naturally towards accountancy, so it is interesting to see that the relevance of accountancy to the subject of their degree was a motivator for nearly half of graduates. However, recruiters recognise the need for balance and variety in teams; they don't want a company of clones. They realise that graduates from disciplines other than business, finance, science and engineering have valuable skills and qualities.

What attracts you to accountancy? Why do you think it would suit you? Perhaps you are unsure that it would? This book should help you become more informed about the profession as a whole.

To conclude, the book will focus on how the profession is optimistic about its future in this rapidly changing world, and how accountancy is likely to remain the career of choice for many of our most talented and ambitious graduates.

To give you some insider knowledge about what it is like to train as an accountant, there are case studies throughout the book from accountants who have been in the same position you are in now, along with profiles from training providers and relevant accountancy organisations.

1

The accounting profession

What is accountancy?

Accountancy is an ancient profession, with the earliest records found in Mesopotamia dating back over 7,000 years. As business evolved, so did the sophistication of accounting records and financial statements. In the first instance records were purely for the business person's own interest, such as simple records of crop and herd growth, but by the fourteenth century in northern Italy, double-entry bookkeeping emerged, recording investments from multiple parties for wider and more varied stakeholders. This necessitated the introduction of accounting systems and records. For internal uses this meant management accounting – the basis for commercial and operational decision-making – while financial accounting developed for external interested parties and shareholders, providing more structured reports for banks, economists, investors and creditors. Later, controls were introduced in the form of external regulation and neutral attestation, or auditing.

Nowadays we all act as accountants in some way in our everyday lives. We manage our personal finances – saving and checking receipts against our bank statements and logging incomings and outgoings. If we do not study and balance our earnings against our outgoings, we might create an inaccurate picture of our financial situation and overstretch ourselves, until we're pulled up by the bank.

In its basic terms, accountancy involves recording, collating, summarising, interpreting and communicating financial information. It is the 'language of business' and it underlies all stages, conveying details about a company's broader economic resources and viability, and pinpointing which parts are more and less profitable. It starts with one set of accountants preparing the accounts, then a second set, the internal auditors, check them to ensure accuracy and compliance with legislation. A third group, the external auditors, then provides an independent rubber stamp of accuracy, or of 'true and fair' representation. Of course, should things go wrong, there could even be a fourth contingent that comes in to save or liquidate the business. Business problems tend to be diagnosed in accountancy terms and therefore remedies are proposed in terms of accounting solutions and technologies, arguably fuelling the demand for yet more accountants!

Accountants need to be very commercially aware, with quantitative, logical and analytical ability and training in finance, law and tax. In-house accountants may prepare profit and loss statements and provide data for annual reports. They may control and oversee payroll, billing and invoicing, or advise on tax, pension schemes, contracts and budgets. They may also contribute ideas about operational efficiency or strategic direction and investments. Accountants are trained to employ structured accounting techniques to pinpoint high-margin or loss-making activities. These techniques are vital to the firm's successful operation. External accountants act more like consultants and inspectors, policing to ensure that nothing fraudulent or irregular is happening and suggesting how the firm could make or save more money or pay less tax, while remaining within the framework of the law.

Where do accountants work?

The answer to this question is anywhere and everywhere. There is certainly no typical employer, but the three main sectors can be categorised as follows:

1. Public Practice (independent accountancy firms offering professional services)

2. industry and commerce (businesses)

3. non-commercial organisations (public sector and not-for-profit bodies).

Public Practice

There are about 5,000 professional or Public Practice firms in the UK. These are predominantly accountancy firms that offer audit, professional and consultancy services to fee-paying, public limited and private company clients. Chartered (ACA) accountants and also chartered certified (ACCA) accountants generally work in Public Practice, with smaller numbers of chartered management (CIMA) accountants and chartered public finance (CIPFA) accountants working in particular divisions and specialisms. The accountancy services they offer can largely be divided into audit, tax and advisory. 'Advisory' comprises everything not related to audit and tax, such as mergers and acquisitions, corporate finance, performance improvement, risk and so on.

The Big Four

The largest of these Public Practice firms – PricewaterhouseCoopers (PwC), Deloitte, KPMG and Ernst & Young – are commonly referred to collectively as the 'Big Four' (see Table 2, p. 9). These handle the vast majority of audits for publicly traded companies and large private companies. Each one is actually a network of global firms, which share a common name, brand and quality, and which are coordinated by their central body (which does not itself practise accountancy or own or control the firm). Many of the founders of these firms were early presidents of the Institute of Chartered Accountants in England and Wales (ICAEW): William Welch Deloitte, Arthur Cooper, Sir William Peat and Frederick Whinney. There were originally eight major players, but a series of mergers and amalgamations gradually led these firms to evolve into four huge entities.

How the 'Big Eight' became the 'Big Four'

The Big Four evolved from an original 'Big Eight'. Until 1987, the 'Big Eight' were:

- Arthur Andersen

- Arthur Young & Co.

- Coopers & Lybrand

- Ernst & Whinney; until 1979, Ernst & Ernst in the US and Whinney Murray in the UK

- Deloitte, Haskins & Sells; until 1978, Haskins & Sells in the US and Deloitte & Co. in the UK

- Peat Marwick Mitchell & Co.; later Peat Marwick, and then KPMG

- Price Waterhouse

- Touche Ross.

During the years 1989 to 1998 there were further mergers, creating the 'Big Six':

- Ernst & Whinney merged with Arthur Young to form Ernst & Young

- Deloitte, Haskins & Sells merged with Touche Ross to form Deloitte Touche Tohmatsu.

Further amalgamations during 1998 to 2001 whittled it down again to the 'Big Five':

- Price Waterhouse merged with Coopers & Lybrand to form PricewaterhouseCoopers.

Involvement in the 2001 Enron scandal resulted in the (since overturned) conviction and demise of Arthur Andersen, leaving only the Big Four.

The Big Four alone employ approximately 64% (nearly 47,000) of the accountants working in Public Practice, leaving just 34% (nearly 27,000) to work in middle-tier or smaller high-street practices, or as sole traders. There are some other very large firms outside the Big Four, but it is hard for them to grow significantly because all but one of the FTSE 100 companies and 240 of the companies in the FTSE 250 are said to be audited by Big Four firms. There is often debate and controversy about the power and monopoly of such audit oligopolists.

Often top graduates aspire to work in one of these firms, perhaps because they are so competitive and prestigious, not to mention the generous remuneration (in London), and the possibility of golden hellos/settlement packages (typically £1,000 to £1,500, and perhaps even £1 million at senior levels). Training and qualification with a Big Four practice does hold kudos and may even be seen as a requirement in a job's person specification. However, stop to consider whether these environments would really suit you best or whether you may in fact prefer, or be better suited to, the cosier ethos and more balanced lifestyle of a smaller or middle-tier practice (see Chapter 3 for more on this).

TABLE 2: The Big Four Public Practice firms, UK, 2011

Firm	UK revenues (2011)	Increase in UK revenue 2010–11	Employees	Headquarters
PwC (PricewaterhouseCoopers)	£2,461m	5.5%	905 UK partners (125 female) 14,973 employees 2,670 trainees 40 UK offices	US
Deloitte Touche Tohmatsu	£2,098m	7.4%	706 UK partners (99 female) 13,075 employees 2,020 trainees 38 UK offices	UK
KPMG	£1,707m	7%	579 UK partners (86 female) 10,150 employees 2,088 trainees 22 UK offices	Netherlands
Ernst & Young	£1,465m	8%	527 UK partners (95 female) 9,239 employees 1,328 trainees 23 UK offices	UK

PricewaterhouseCoopers

The PricewaterhouseCoopers (PwC; www.pwc.com) global professional services network is the largest revenue-generating practice in the UK and employs over 169,000 people in offices in 771 cities across 158 different countries. In 2011, PwC regained its title as the largest global accounting firm from Deloitte after slipping to second in 2010. PwC employs nearly 15,000 people in the UK and has 40 offices nationally. Around 40% of the FTSE 100 companies are audited by PwC, substantially more than any of the other Big Four firms.

PwC is the largest graduate recruiter, taking on more than 1,000 graduates every year in the UK. In 2011 it saw the largest spring intake in graduate recruits: 209 joined PwC UK in April. This was a high number as PwC also has a September intake which sees the higher number in graduate recruits. In 2010 it introduced a new scheme to its graduate recruitment programme, Inspired Talent. The focus was to open up its graduate scheme to those who may not have had the academic success needed for *it*, but who had achieved other great things. The scheme looks to widen the talent pool by challenging the idea that academic success is the best way to identify applicants who will be successful in the workplace, and therefore it aims to reduce the current reliance placed on academic qualifications by many graduate recruiters.

The firm's name stems from the merger of Price Waterhouse and Coopers & Lybrand in 1998, but rebranding in 2010 gave birth to PwC.

For the last eight years, PwC has been voted first in *The Times'* Top 100 Graduate Employers and it is ranked fifth in *The Sunday Times'* Best Big Companies to Work For listing in 2012, the highest ranking among professional services firms for the year. PwC has also received technical accolades, including Top Professional Services Adviser of 2010 at the Insurance Day Awards, UK Transfer Pricing Firm of the Year 2011 and European Transfer Pricing Firm of the Year 2011 at the International Tax Review Awards in May 2011, Employee Benefits Consultant of the Year, Pensions Covenant Review Provider of the Year at the *Financial Times* Pension & Investment Provider Awards 2012, and Pensions Scheme Accountant of the Year at the Professional Pensions Awards 2012. Also named Upper Middle Market M&A (mergers and acquisitions) Adviser of the Year in the Acquisitions Monthly Awards, the company is said to 'dominate in audit and restructuring'.

Service lines are separated into:

- advisory (performance improvement, strategy, corporate finance, recovery and so on).

- assurance

- tax advisory

PwC has broad industry specialisms of:

- consumer and industrial products and services

- financial services

- technology, information, communications and entertainment

- infrastructure, government and utilities

- private company services.

It is an interesting fact that, since 1934, PwC has acted as tabulator and certifier of votes for the Academy Awards, but, unfortunately, the company may also be remembered for its slap on the wrist from the House of Lords in 2011 for not identifying the flaws and risks in the business model of Northern Rock, the bank that was nationalised in 2008 after suffering a run in the credit crisis.

In the financial year 2011, PwC's community contribution came to £10.3 million. Supported by its Matched Giving Programme and Volunteering Awards Scheme, 4,226 of its UK staff gave 50,206 hours to help out with a wide range of community activities either during work hours or in their own time.

PwC is committed to improving its sustainability: it has taken a pivotal role in shaping the sustainability debate, and was heavily involved in COP 16 in Cancun (the United Nations' Climate Change Conference). The organisation leads the Climate and Development Knowledge Network, and has written up a thorough survey on the low-carbon economy, *Appetite for Change*, and the *Low Carbon Economy Index* report. Discerning graduates are increasingly asking about such issues at interview, and PwC may therefore be particularly appealing if you are interested in 'green' issues.

'Word on the street' suggests that PwC is rather bureaucratic and corporate. The opportunity for progression is limited and the promotion structure affords little flexibility until you have been there more than four years. Salary may be affected by your department's success, and visibility by the importance of your clients; in other words, it may not be a meritocracy. PwC employees are sometimes described as arrogant or elitist. Perhaps this is because the company aims to employ the best. However, the workforce is very diverse and there are good opportunities for women, and it is said to have a strong training scheme and a supportive culture. The dress code may also be rather more relaxed, with smart casual being preferred to suits at times. If you are competitive and believe you are the best, the PwC working culture may suit you.

Deloitte

Deloitte (www.deloitte.com) is a member of the global professional services group Deloitte Touche Tohmatsu (DTTL). DTTL is a private company established in the UK and limited by guarantee. In 2010, it just nudged ahead of PwC to become the largest private professional services network in the world based on aggregate member firm revenues and headcount (rather than UK revenues). However, in 2011 PwC regained the leadership position as the largest accounting firm in the world after publishing revenues $400 million more than Deloitte's. Around 20% of the FTSE 100 companies are audited by Deloitte, approximately 20% fewer than PwC audits.

Deloitte now has 182,000 members of staff across 150 countries with plans for further expansion. It has 38 offices in the UK, employing 13,075 people and recruiting over 1,400 graduates and undergraduates each year, through schemes such as its graduate programme, industrial placements and summer vacation programmes.

Deloitte's main service offerings are divided into:

- **audit (including accounting and payroll solutions and enterprise risk services)**

- consulting (including actuarial and pensions services and human capital)

- corporate finance (including forensic and dispute services and specialist services)

- tax (for businesses, employers, individuals and entrepreneurs).

Deloitte has performed well in recent industry awards. In 2011 the company received 12 awards at the seventh annual International Tax Review European Tax Awards as well as two awards at the LexisNexis 2011 Taxation Awards. In 2010 it won nine awards, including Asia Indirect Tax Firm of the Year.

Additionally, Deloitte was listed sixteenth in *The Sunday Times'* Best Big Companies to Work For in 2011 and voted second in *The Times'* Top 100 Graduate Employers in 2011 for the sixth consecutive year. Deloitte is committed to diversity, as reflected in its Global Retention of Women (GROW) Council, the Global Diversity and Inclusion Community of Practice, and its recognition of International Women's Day. In 2010, Deloitte was recognised as having the best flexible working and family friendly policies and excellent flexible career opportunities, appearing in the workingmums.co.uk top employer awards. Deloitte was also listed among the top 50 employers for women in *The Times'* Top Companies for Women 2011, so it's one to consider if you are planning to be a working parent. Also, at the Race for Opportunity Awards, the Deloitte Employability Initiative won the prize for Collaboration and Partnership.

Deloitte21 is a Deloitte network-wide global initiative to help disadvantaged young people acquire the education and skills required to thrive in the economy of the twenty-first century. The firm is also committed to sustainability and people issues. In addition, Deloitte (UK) was a sponsor of the 2012 Olympic and Paralympic Games and the only one of the Big Four firms to have a specialist sports business group.

What do people in the industry say? Deloitte is said to have a friendly, practical, 'work hard, play hard' team culture, with strong two-way communication encouraged and practised. It professes to be committed to diversity, but may not actually be as diverse as other firms. Arrogance is again a criticism levelled at Deloitte. There are said to be early promotion opportunities but training often needs to be self-initiated. Perks are good and include interest-free loans, moving expenses, private gym, and dinner and taxis provided when you work late. Deloitte has the reputation of being the most innovative of the Big Four, so if you like to think creatively, this could perhaps be the firm for you.

KPMG

KPMG (www.kpmgcareers.co.uk) – the result of five mergers of European firms – employs over 138,000 people operating in 150 countries (10,150 in the UK), and has a network of 144 offices globally (22 in the UK). KPMG works with 71% of the FTSE 350 companies, and audits 24% of the FTSE 100 firms.

KPMG service lines are broken into:

- audit (the firm is particularly strong in this area)

- tax (business, personal and Asian)

- advisory (corporate finance, risk, forensic, IT, restructuring, recruitment, etc.)

- other (Global China Practice).

KPMG also prides itself on its awards for people and technical excellence. It is consistently in the top 10 of *The Sunday Times'* Best Big Companies to Work For, ranked eighth in 2012, rising one spot from ninth in 2011. In 2009 the company received a special lifetime achievement award in view of this. In 2011, KPMG was ranked third in *The Times'* Top 100 Graduate Employers survey, up one from 2010, and named World's Best Outsourcing Advisers.

KPMG is the only member of the Big Four firms to have a full-time dedicated professional qualification training (PQT) team. This consists of 17 people (most of whom have studied the qualifications themselves) who provide help and support to graduates throughout their training.

In recent years, KPMG has put a greater focus on the environment and demonstrates this by allowing all its staff half a day of firm time to volunteer in their local community each month. In 2011 alone, 39% of their staff contributed 41,200 hours to communities through volunteering, and the firm's total community investment rose to £11.1 million. The firm has also won several Giving Something Back Awards too. In 2011, KPMG introduced the BRIGHT programme. This is an initiative for corporate social responsibility. The programme encourages members of staff to use their skills and talents to either act locally or globally. BRIGHT ideas are submitted on how these skills can be used to help social and environmental challenges that are being faced. Since the introduction of the programme, 10,000 members of staff have given over 77,000 hours to volunteering.

KPMG is said to have a relaxed working environment, where there is early responsibility and varied work. There are good progression opportunities and members of staff are supported well. However, a casual dress policy isn't incorporated at KPMG. Importance is given to diversity, and KPMG is a good firm for female workers. Remote working is actively encouraged, and the contributions of employees are recognised and rewarded via competitive salaries, plus a bonus scheme that reflects individual performance and also allows everyone to share in KPMG's success.

Ernst & Young

Ernst & Young (www.ey.com) is one of the longest established of the Big Four. Ernst & Young LLP is the UK member of Ernst & Young Global. It employs more than 150,000 people across 695 offices, providing professional services in 140 countries, and has a very impressive revenue and client list. In the UK, Ernst & Young employs 9,239 staff in 23 offices. Around 17% of the FTSE 100 companies are audited by Ernst & Young.

The company's service lines are categorised as:

- advisory services (actuarial, IT risk and assurance risk, and performance improvement)

- assurance

- tax services

- transaction advisory services.

Ernst & Young has recently been awarded a number of accolades, including topping Stonewall's 2012 list of the best 100 employers, which showcases Britain's top employers for gay, lesbian and bisexual staff. In 2011, Ernst & Young's UK operations were awarded the Carbon Trust Standard; this recognises organisations that make real carbon reductions. Also, the firm was awarded the Race of Opportunity Award in recognition of its Black and Minority Ethnic Leadership Programme.

Ernst & Young remained at number 10 in *The Times'* Top 100 Graduate Employers in 2011, and was also ranked tenth in the *Guardian's* UK 300 (the top 300 graduate employers) in 2011. However, it is the only one of the Big Four that does not make it into *The Sunday Times'* Best Big Companies to Work For 2012.

In 2011, Ernst & Young was three times a winner at the Scottish Accountancy Awards, including winning the Best Large Firm Award, and won two Management Consultancies Association Awards for Public Sector Outsourcing and Change Management in the Public Sector. In 2010, Ernst & Young was recognised for its commitment to corporate social responsibility (CSR), landing three Business in the Community Awards for Excellence, as well as technical awards for tax and pensions.

Ernst & Young has been committed for 17 years to sponsoring the arts, including gallery and museum exhibitions, as well as educational programmes for children. Its well-known Entrepreneur of the Year Awards has been running for over two decades and celebrates entrepreneurship in the UK and internationally.

Ernst & Young received a CommunityMark in 2008, in recognition of the commitment it has to UK communities. Through its Profitunity! scheme, students from 10 universities raised £68,000 for The Prince's Trust, of which Ernst & Young is a gold patron. The scheme focused on helping young people achieve their potential in the areas of education and entrepreneurship.

In September 2011, Ernst & Young was announced as a tier 2 official sponsor and the provider of professional services to the Olympic Games to be held in Rio in 2016.

Ernst & Young would no doubt prefer to forget its involvement in the Anglo Irish Bank hidden loans controversy, in which it failed to detect some large, irregular loans to the bank's chairman during its audit. In 2009, the bank was criticised by politicians, resulting in a 99% drop in share price, and in turn necessitating a bailout by the Irish government. The chief executive officer (CEO) at the Central Bank of Ireland commented that 'a layperson would expect that issues of this nature and this magnitude would have been picked up'. It cost the Irish people about £4,800 per head.

Ernst & Young is said to have a strong reputation for corporate finance. It is also committed to CSR, people and diversity issues, with generous maternity and paternity provisions. People in the profession say the culture of Ernst & Young is particularly friendly and liberal. New, open-plan offices are being introduced – not even the partners have their own offices – and there is a 'hot desk' policy meaning that you can change desk daily. Both of these are intended to promote a relaxed, supportive and open climate. There is a roughly even male/female mix and flexible working is possible, but salaries may be slightly lower than in the other three firms. However, if you want to reach middle management rapidly, then Ernst & Young could be for you. Equally, globalisation is a reality at Ernst & Young, and it is said that many choose the firm for its strong international opportunities.

Does the size of the Public Practice firm make any difference?

The vast majority of chartered accountants train in Public Practice, and graduate training for chartered accountancy qualifications (ACA) in this sector involves securing a mandatory three-year salaried training contract with one of over 2,200 providers in the UK and internationally. These are accredited by the ICAEW or its Scottish or Irish equivalents (Institute of Chartered Accountants of Scotland (ICAS) or in Ireland (ICAI)).

Depending on academic qualifications, on the qualification wanted, and on the specialism or service division preferred, chartered certified (ACCA) accountants, chartered management (CIMA) accountants and chartered public finance (CIPFA) accountants may also secure such training contracts with these large 'audit' firms, or with one of many other smaller professional practices. Obviously, not everyone can work for one of the Big Four firms, but with training and experience in industry, accountants may move into Public Practice post-qualification.

The standard of training should be consistent whether you go for a large, medium or small employer, because the quality demanded for professional body approval is very high. Therefore, the choice of training employer will be largely a matter of your own preference, plus the employer's requirements in terms of academic credentials and experience.

Large international firms

In large firms, you are likely to be assigned to a specialist area, such as audit (which is the main career destination for most trainees), corporate finance or tax, whereas a smaller firm might offer broader, across-the-board experience, although in some cases smaller firms can be very specialised, for instance in forensic accounting. Larger firms obviously have more openings – the Big Four have many thousands of trainees – and they are largely situated in bigger cities and towns. You are not, therefore, restricted to working in London, or even in the UK. The clients of the larger firms tend to be FTSE 100 companies and multinationals.

Starting salaries may be higher, but working days will be long, stretching well into the small hours during busy periods. Some firms have a tough 'up or out' policy, and it is common to be expected to leave should you fail the professional examinations – repeated retakes are often not acceptable – or should you not progress appropriately and it becomes evident that you are not seen as partner material. However, it can be exciting and challenging to join and work with a cohort of intelligent, ambitious and thrusting accountancy trainees who are on the fast track together. Table 3 shows how many trainees of each major professional body are currently studying with Big Four firms.

TABLE 3: Numbers of trainees in the Big Four, 2012

	Total trainees	ICAEW	ICAS	ACCA	CIMA	CIPFA
PwC	2,769	2,397	206	166	0	0
Deloitte	2,161	1,716	128	0	317	n/a
KPMG	2,241	1,414	522	121	122	36
Ernst & Young	1,728	278	925	228	297	0

Training and career pathways tend to be structured. It may take longer to secure a senior role in a larger firm, but then there may be fewer management tiers. In both large and smaller organisations it should be possible to make executive director within nine to 12 years and senior executive partner within 10 to 15 years.

Medium-sized firms

These tend to be firms with a network of offices and regional practices and varying numbers of employees and partners, but the client list may be no less impressive than that of large firms and may include independent, international and 'big name' businesses. In medium-sized practices, you may have greater responsibility more quickly and there may be a better team spirit.

The Big Four firms have the resources and clients to attract and cream off the most talented graduates; however, those training in smaller practices may eventually gravitate to the bigger practices post-qualification because of the higher salaries and greater opportunities. The reverse can also occur, when disillusionment sets in at a bigger firm and people seek a different cultural setting or specialism, or perhaps a more niche clientele.

Medium-sized practices should be large enough to cope with a diverse client range, and small enough to still be friendly and to afford scope for individuality. There may be less choice in your starting point: all graduates may start in audit, for example. With somewhat smaller client businesses, audits may take as little as one or two weeks compared with the six to nine months that audits take for the big clients of larger firms. At medium-sized firms you may be able to do most of the work yourself rather than just taking responsibility for a small part of the process.

As with large firms, training is likely to include internal support from the training division, internal technical training and external professional training from an accredited provider. The training provider should liaise closely with the company to ensure that trainees are on track for examinations, and advise the firm should additional assistance be needed. Regular feedback may be provided by a personal mentor, and, if applicable, you may have six-monthly reviews with your counselling partner regarding initial professional development (IPD), the required ICAEW log of practical experience.

Small firms

Smaller firms tend to offer a more personal approach to their clients, who can include a wide range of people and businesses – individuals, partnerships and small business clients. Some people find it particularly rewarding to advise and work more closely with freelancers, self-employed professionals, business owners and start-ups, and the work is likely to cover all aspects of accountancy. In general practice, you usually work in a small team on accounts' preparation, end-of-year audit and tax matters, and you are quickly familiarised with the key issues for small business success such as managing tax and financial affairs, controlling and reducing costs, improving systems and generating growth and wealth. Small-firm accountants may be more able to recognise individual differences and to assure a client that their needs are being fully understood and professionally and accurately addressed. Smaller firms still need to invest in training, systems and software to keep fees competitive while providing quality services.

Clients may include high-street estate agents, restaurateurs, travel agents, and all manner of retailers, as well as local builders and property developers, recruitment, media and information service companies, and many professionals, including career consultants, pharmacists, physiotherapists, doctors and surveyors. Smaller firms may pride themselves on being active and accessible members of their clients' teams and having a high client retention rate.

You are likely to enjoy a more balanced lifestyle in a small high-street practice, with little if any travel. Working in a small firm means you won't be confined to a big town and you will have more options available to you. You will gain experience across the board, therefore widening your expertise more rapidly, although there are some small specialised practices as well. Of course, you may even aspire to opening your own small practice in the future.

Industry and commerce

Here, you would work internally in the finance department of a commercial company, in industries including retail, telecommunications, transport, fast-moving consumer goods (FMCG), banking and manufacturing. You may train in-house; the favoured qualifications are often CIMA or ACCA, although there are an increasing number of ACA training opportunities becoming available. You may move into an in-house role in Public Practice post-qualification. In many cases, large companies and most small- and medium-sized firms will fund study and provide leave for trainee accountants to pursue professional qualifications. Obviously, studying on the job will provide you with valuable experience and industry insight.

In-house accountants budget for and control monies coming into and going out of the firm, in addition to considering operational efficiency, or strategic direction, funding and investments. They might work in a generalist role in a smaller firm, or in a more specialised reporting, analysis, control, taxation or corporate finance capacity in a larger organisation.

In-house, you will work with the same colleagues and internal clients, and this may suit you better should you not enjoy regrouping and working with different teams and clients, which may be the case when working for large companies. Within an industry with national and global concerns there may still be some travel involved. You are perhaps also better placed to see the long-term results of your interventions.

Internal accountants may not adhere to the traditional image of the profession. You may be working with a broader range of people, trying to ensure that non-finance colleagues understand the numbers and the implications these may have. An advantage of this sector is that you can choose to work for a company where you have some interest in the line of business, whether it's manufacturing or a service industry. Graduate programmes often involve rotational six-month placements, affording variety and broader commercial experience and insight. As a trainee in manufacturing, you could be thrown straight in, with immediate responsibility for two product lines and two teams reporting directly to you – quite a baptism of fire! From there you might, for example, move to the marketing team as a commercial analyst, evaluating product changes, costings, seasonal promotions and even which products to put in a selection box or gift pack.

A typical day might involve checking correspondence, liaising, meetings and taking conference calls with departmental managers to discuss project budgets, figures and strategy, and preparing financial data for presentations. With time you should have increasing responsibility and ownership of projects and results, working with senior decision-makers across the company, and perhaps even with external parties, subcontractors and stakeholders. It can be fun to identify, locate and tap the person with the necessary information in a larger company, and to be party to high-level commercial strategy- and decision-making. Internally, you are immediately putting theory into practice, consolidating your learning.

Again, it can be hard to work and study simultaneously, but, as previously stated, study days and exam leave are offered by a number of firms. It helps to be driven, adaptable and capable in time management.

Non-commercial organisations

The public sector includes local and central government, not-for-profit organisations such as charities and non-governmental organisations (NGOs) as well as the NHS and organisations with educational concerns. The public sector was not historically a major trainer of chartered accountants as the pertinent qualification has traditionally been CIPFA, but there are increasing opportunities for trainees. Many accountants, whatever their qualification, transfer into the not-for-profit sector post-qualification or later in their career, when seeking greater work—life balance or when their personal values become more social and altruistic and less focused on material rewards. However, the pay in this sector is not as poor as many think and efficiency is not any less important.

In the public sector, the work involves managing income, for example rent and council tax, and making best use of public funds by advising and working with managers to maximise and improve service provision in accordance with budgets and the needs of the community. There are roles in the public sector similar to those in practice: for example, audit and tax specialists. Again, there are accountants in professional practice who, while not employed by the public sector, have public-sector specialisms as they may deal solely with public sector clients. This way you can have your feet in both camps at once.

This type of work would suit individuals who are more politically and socially focused. While there is not likely to be as much travel in local government, you may need to attend some meetings locally and nationally with partner organisations, funders and colleagues in other organisations. There may also be job opportunities abroad with the EU, or in NGOs and development organisations.

Interestingly, accountants have moved increasingly towards the public and not-for-profit sectors. This may be because we have entered an era of 'do-gooding', philosophy and ethics, or because people are seeking greater security and balance in insecure economic times, not that the public sector has been safe from the cuts recently. Fortunately, it has always been considered beneficial to bring commercial thinking to the non-commercial sector.

What are the main roles in accountancy?

In the professional practice, business, industry and non-commercial sectors discussed above, there is a great variety of potential roles, ranging from analytical and policing, to advisory and control, and to strategic functions. These days, there seems to be much more movement between sectors and roles; indeed, one of the joys of accountancy is the variety, as well as the scope for constant change and the challenge it affords.

Financial accounting

Financial accountants can work in Public Practice and internally in companies. They produce the summary financial statements and reports required predominantly by external stakeholders and agencies, which include stockholders, stockbrokers, banks, suppliers, government agencies and media groups, but obviously they might be of value internally too. Information is taken from accounting records and published at least annually for the benefit of interested parties. Financial accounting can also involve forecasting and developing projections, and perhaps revising accounting and reporting policies.

The key responsibilities might include period-end reporting, possibly within tight deadlines, management of the preliminary and year-end audits in collaboration with the firm's auditors, management and review of budgets, implementation of controls processes, and mentoring of colleagues and associates.

Month end

- Preparation of all month-end journals including prepayments, depreciation, provisions and accruals

- Monthly payroll reconciliation and query resolution, bank reconciliations and currency account conversions

- Completion of monthly financial close

- Reconciliation and sign-off of all balance sheet control accounts to month-end deadlines

- Production of financial and management reports, with commentary

- Production of actual/budget comparisons, investigating variances as necessary

Compliance

- Filing within statutory deadlines all tax and fiscal requirements

- Responsibility for local and international VAT (or equivalent) records and returns

Audit

- Producing accounts with backed-up audit files

- Managing all local audits

- Ensuring complete, accurate local fiscal reporting within deadlines

- Providing support and documentation for tax advisers for annual returns and compliance

Additional responsibilities

- Monitoring local cashflows

- Providing group cover as required

- Working effectively with, and supporting, all members of the organisation (this may include staff management)

Financial accounting is quite similar to the role of an information officer, but it does afford scope for personal judgements and estimates in line with 'generally accepted accounting principles' (GAAP) and the 'convention of objectivity' in accounting. As with taxation (which is discussed later), you can look at things in different ways but you tend to be dealing with historical rather than current data. The work can be quite retrospective, although new technology is making the available data more up to date.

Unlike in management accountancy and financial analysis, you would not typically be considering non-monetary factors such as business competition, the impact of new technical innovations, loyalty and competence of staff or even currency changes. The work involves working with aggregates rather than digging into the detail of, for example, which products may be performing better. It is more about reporting than changing things; management accountants, financial controllers and directors are the people who have more scope to shape how things are done. This could be frustrating if you are more proactive and forward-looking in your style.

Profile: The Chartered Institute of Payroll Professionals

The Chartered Institute of Payroll Professionals (CIPP) is the only Chartered Institute for payroll professionals in the UK and currently has in excess of 5,000 members enjoying a range of benefits.

The advice and support offered by the CIPP are ideal for accountants who wish to offer payroll services to their clients; the CIPP is the leading provider of professional payroll qualifications in the UK. In addition, the CIPP has a pensions faculty delivering qualifications and membership services to those responsible for public sector pensions.

The mission statement of the CIPP is: 'leading payroll and pension professionals through education, membership and recognition'.

Education

The CIPP is the leading provider of qualifications, training and consultancy for payroll professionals in the UK. Our payroll qualifications programme starts at level three and consists of both face-to-face and online development opportunities. Qualifications available are:

- National Payroll Certificates: level three
- Payroll Technician Certificate: level three
- Foundation degree in Payroll Management: level four/five
- BA (Hons) in Applied Business and Management: level six
- MSc in Business and Payroll Management: level seven.

As well as our industry-recognised qualifications, the CIPP boasts a wide range of payroll training courses to increase professional knowledge in specific areas such as statutory payments, termination payments, overpayment recovery and changes to legislation.

Membership

The CIPP is the only chartered body for people working in payroll in the UK, and has a separate pensions faculty to represent public sector pensions professionals. The CIPP has an excellent position within government to represent our members' views. This also means we can keep you abreast of changes in legislation through a number of communications channels, including:

- *News On Line*: a weekly e-newsletter
- *Payroll Professional* magazine, issued ten months a year
- an advisory service: a helpline you can call during office hours
- members-only sections of the website to network and discuss topical issues.

Recognition

The CIPP is working hard to increase recognition of the importance of payroll in business, and we achieved chartered status for the profession in 2010. The policy team is now representing members' views at over 60 government consultation forums – which highlights that HM Revenue & Customs (HMRC) and other government departments recognise the important part that payroll plays in the UK economy.

Find out more about the CIPP by visiting www.cipp.org.uk, emailing info@cipp.org.uk or calling 0121 712 1000 and quoting reference number WIA2012.

Case study

Michelle Sutton, payroll manager for The Body Shop

What is your career background?

I joined the payroll department for Tesco Stores Ltd in February 2001, as a Payroll Administrator. I quickly progressed to Payroll and Benefits Call Centre Executive, followed by Payroll Supervisor, and then headed a Payroll Control and Audit Team, which involved my making many visits to India, to support the offshore teams. I was later offered a role as Assistant Manager for Payroll, and in 2007 my family and I moved to Bangalore, India, where I set up an offshore Payroll Control Team and spent a year supporting the payroll operations for Tesco in India.

Once I returned from Bangalore, my role with Tesco was made redundant; I successfully gained payroll manager roles at MITIE, Catalent Pharma Solutions and Integreon Managed Solutions. I am currently the Payroll Manager for The Body Shop International plc (which is owned by L'Oréal).

What were your reasons for obtaining a payroll qualification?

When I left Tesco I quickly realised employers wanted CIPP-qualified applicants. I felt that having the qualification would better my career prospects and I was ready for a new challenge.

What did you enjoy the most about your studies?

I enjoyed meeting other like-minded professionals from other companies; I built some strong relationships, and I keep in touch with many of the students I met during our study years. We provided support to each other during assignment deadlines, throwing ideas around and encouraging each other. I realised the importance of attending module review days and tutorials, not only for the informative discussions and sharing of information but also to catch up with the other students and share our experiences.

What were the main challenges?

I found the main challenge during my studies was the impact on my personal time, especially with a family. You do have to dedicate a lot of time and energy to achieve good grades, so there is pressure when you are working full-time and completing further education. However, I personally believe this is well worth the time and effort spent.

What do you think are the benefits of getting a payroll qualification?

This is such a recognised qualification that it offers a clear advantage when applying for roles in the payroll/pensions sector. I have found my employers trust my advice, and I enjoy being empowered to run the payroll operations with the support of the senior management team.

What advice would you give to someone who is considering doing a payroll qualification?

I would absolutely encourage anyone to do this qualification. Since qualifying myself, I have encouraged two of my payroll administrators to start the course; one has recently started year 1, and another passed the APEL interview and has gone in at year 2 stage.

In what ways have your studies brought about a change in your perception of your role and that of payroll?

I realise it's not just about paying people; it's about delivering a first-class level of service to our customers and feeding into the broader goals of the business via an integrated human resource (HR) rewards strategy. Payroll can help people feel valued and contribute to staff satisfaction and retention.

Auditing and assurance

The majority of Public Practice ACA trainees 'do their time' in auditing at the start of their career, but there are also internal audit roles. The reality of auditing is that it is technical and lacking in variety. The work often involves long hours and substantial travel, which could take up to 90% of your time when you're not studying, although one trainee had been lucky enough to have never had more than a two-hour commute. Audit involves retrospective, independent tests and checks, usually as a team on the client's premises, assessing the accuracy, honesty and risk of an organisation's financial situation. Do company and bank records match? Do employees really exist? How much is stock really worth? Most accounting firms will have developed a set audit methodology based on generally accepted auditing standards (GAAS).

Auditing can be seen as policing, but it has a consultancy or 'value-added' element as well, in that recommendations may be made regarding how business processes, procedures, systems and controls might be improved, perhaps 'selling' the client additional services. Auditors ensure that monies that go in and come out of a company are recorded and processed accurately. Auditing is often what people think of when they think of accountancy, but only around 30% of qualified accountants work in this field.

Key responsibilities might include:

- developing and maintaining positive relationships with clients and colleagues – you may need great diplomacy in situations where there is disagreement between the client and the auditor

- collating data, and scrutinising and analysing spreadsheets

- checking company accounts

- testing financial control systems, according to set models, tools and techniques

- identifying and assessing levels of financial risk within organisations

- ensuring that financial reports and records are accurate and reliable (referring to original entries and reading between the lines)

- ensuring that assets are safeguarded

- identifying if and where processes are flawed or failing, and advising on changes to be made

- preparing reports, commentaries and financial statements

- liaising with managers and presenting findings and recommendations

- using in-depth knowledge of accounting legislation to ensure compliance with procedures, policies, legislation and regulations

- undertaking reviews of wages.

By its very nature, auditing may not be seen as being all that exciting as you are mostly just checking invoices, accounts, data and controls, but there are people who love the profession. Some people say it is varied due to the clients, although at the most junior level it can be quite administrative – you will be arranging couriers, photocopying and clearing up. You do need to be patient and accept that you will need to learn and work your way up from the bottom. In large, structured firms, you may have several set tasks in the first year and then several set tasks the following year, so you will simply be duplicating a process with different clients. You may feel out of your depth initially but once you understand how it works it may become tedious. However, using your initiative and asking for something more challenging may be all that is required should you begin to feel jaded!

The ethos will differ depending on with whom, and for whom, you are working. You may have a micromanaging boss, or one who is hands-off. Some managers will let you go when your work is done; others will make you stay until everyone is finished. The team you work with could be fun, but they may be people you have never previously met; you do have to adapt readily to new people and environments. Obviously, this can be a good learning experience and you might consciously study your managers' techniques and body language, whether good or bad. You may make friends and then never see them again, which of course is not a bad thing if you did not gel. Some clients resent your presence and therefore will be uncooperative and try to make life difficult for you. This is perhaps why people skills are so often emphasised by recruiters; you may need to charm clients into helping and providing necessary information! January to March tends to be the busiest period, when there may be considerably longer working hours.

The amount of study you will undertake while completing your professional qualifications will vary according to the organisation. You may do 9a.m. until 4p.m. in college with up to an hour's homework and perhaps the same length day at weekends to keep up. It can be very intense. It may be quite difficult to grasp until applied in practice, and everyone would admit that working and studying is hard. Some firms require their employees to be in college for 18 weeks in the first year to cover all 12 'knowledge' modules, and if you are lucky your employer may give you five days' study leave for each week spent in college. In the first three months, you could expect to spend a month at college, three weeks on training courses and five weeks in a hotel, a bonus if you enjoy variety. Whatever the task, remember to be patient, stick to the job in hand and do it with confidence and enthusiasm.

While people skills are emphasised, the reality is that you may spend about 10 hours per day looking at a computer screen. Some people will take an hour for lunch while others will work straight through, but hours will vary depending on the job. Some trainees claim to have never had to stay beyond 5.45p.m., but remember there could be substantial travel time on top of this. IT skills are crucial as you might start with a laptop and then you may begin to acquire various secure USB drives and wireless internet cards. The first two hours of the day may well be spent trying to access the network! You can be posted anywhere nationally, which means that you could be out of the office, and away from home, for months at a time. You will be housed in a local hotel, but, given that clients may be situated outside the city, a car may be an advantage.

Despite the recent recession, auditing is still a secure, well-paid job that can lead to more exciting and challenging work in the future. During your training, you will be working with the brightest and most ambitious people and can build lasting friendships with your fellow trainees. You will also gain a solid grounding in accountancy that may expose you to many different companies and industries. Many people do actually enjoy their time spent in the auditing profession and the work they encounter.

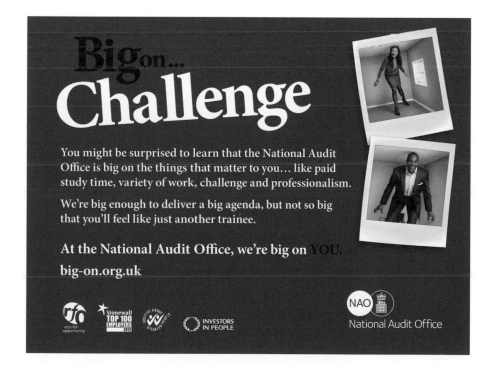

Profile: The National Audit Office

Challenge

The work of the National Audit Office (NAO) covers the whole of central government spending. It is complex, varied and challenging. Our financial audit work involves auditing 458 accounts a year, representing hundreds of billions of pounds. We also publish around 60 high-profile Value for Money reports a year, which often hit the headlines. It's a great time to join us with all the attention being paid to improving the delivery of public services and achieving good value for the taxpayer.

Impact

Our financial audit and Value for Money work helps save the country millions of pounds a year (more than £1 billion in 2011–12) and helps to improve public services. We have a great reputation for professionalism, rigour and judgement.

Success

The NAO's pass rates for the ICAEW exams are consistently around 10% above the national average. We provide generous study leave, relevant work experience that allows you to put what you study into practice, and an excellent system of support.

Careers

You will benefit from a range of ongoing career development opportunities designed to equip you with the skills you need to develop into a potential leader of tomorrow. Our very best people advance rapidly and a great many of the people who qualify with us choose to stay with the NAO.

Life

We take the welfare and well-being of our staff seriously, with a range of policies to support you and to ensure that you have a life outside work as well as inside. We are committed to diversity.

So, where can I find out more and apply?

Visit big-on.org.uk to find out everything you need to know about our student schemes and to complete the online application process.

Key facts

What we do: The NAO scrutinises government spending on behalf of Parliament.

Number of employees: 880

The scheme: Professional training scheme leading to an accountancy qualification (ICAEW)

Starting salary: London £27,432, Newcastle £21,825 + benefits

Number of graduate vacancies: Approximately 70 in London, 10 in Newcastle

Minimum requirements: A minimum of a 2.i in any degree discipline and at least 300 UCAS points

Application deadline: 31 December 2012

Contact: HR team – 020 7798 7227, HR_Service_Desk@nao.gsi.gov.uk

Case study

Rachel Savage, audit specialist at PwC

Why did you choose auditing?

I was lucky enough to get a summer placement with PwC and from that was offered a job. What attracted me in the first place was the variety of the role – you can look after large listed clients and family-run businesses at the same time and learn a lot and very different things from both. I also believe it offers an unrivalled grounding in and understanding of businesses, which, coming from a very unrelated degree, I needed. I was also attracted to the chance to work overseas and since starting I have worked on jobs in New York, Chicago and Oregon as well as in most of the UK.

What do you do on a typical day?

I don't think there is a typical day! I tend to get into work early and then it depends on my clients. I spend as much of my time with my clients and my teams as possible, so that means I can be in quite a few different places each day. A core part of my role is coaching the team through the work and then reviewing it. I also spend a lot of time in meetings with the clients and the partners to ensure we are on track.

I also look after one of our social groups in the department so spend time ensuring we are meeting all our internal measures and planning for the next night out, so a bit different from the 'day job'!

How is your work different now from when you first started?

Wow – very different. When you first start you spend blocks of time at each of your clients and are on site all day working through the detail. When you get to senior manager (my level), you have to run between your clients making sure your teams understand what they are doing and ensuring everything is going to plan. I spend a lot more time reviewing work than doing it now and discussing the key aspects of our audit with the client teams.

What are the best and worst bits?

The best bits are definitely when I get to help clients through problems they are facing or in some way help develop the teams I am working with.

The worst bits – probably time sheets and trying to remember where I spend my time each week!

What skills do you need?

You need to be hard-working, able to adapt and apply your skills to different situations and enjoy variety. I think, most importantly, you also need to be able to get on with people. Whenever I say I am an accountant most people think you have to be good with numbers; I think being an auditor means you have to be good with people. You need to be able to talk and build relationships with your clients and coach your teams through the work.

Any other tips?

Like in most jobs, I think you also need to be able to have fun and bring your own personality and opinion to this role.

Taxation

Tax is commonly perceived as being a mundane and complex area to work in, but it depends how you look at it. There are a number of different aspects to the work, including regulatory compliance, corporate governance and more proactive planning. Companies and individuals need to complete and submit annual tax returns and careful and detailed analysis and problem-solving will enable tax specialists to make suggestions for financial restructuring. Their aim is to ensure that clients, both companies and individuals, pay the minimum legally possible. It often saves their clients substantial sums, but it is important that everyone involved understands the implications of legal decisions and contracts.

Tax is quite 'verbal', being as much about law as it is about numbers. The work may have more of a routine in that you have an ongoing relationship with clients and you primarily work from your own office. You can work internally with a large firm or in Public Practice, advising on corporate and personal tax or VAT, or offering consultancy, tax investigation or forensics services.

Some tax specialists work in personal tax compliance, completing returns for high-net-worth individuals with complex personal affairs. Information needs to be carefully organised and classified, and deadlines need to be met. Other specialists work with the trust department by preparing trust accounts and tax returns, inputting information in journals and calculating end-of-year accruals, before presenting them to clients for their signature.

There may also be an opportunity to work in global employer services where you would be advising and managing files on executive remuneration, such as tax on directors' fees and equity-based allowances, and expatriate planning and complex equalisation processes. Additionally, you could be preparing departmental newsletters, articles and brochures.

Then again, you might work in tax depreciation, calculating tax savings for firms due to expenditure on qualifying items such as plant and machinery. Capital allowances for clients are then submitted to HMRC. The work may involve site visits, for example to airports, car dealerships, factories and offices, and taking notes and photographing assets *in situ*, and subsequently referring to these survey results when preparing reports.

On a typical day working in tax you would spend a great deal of time communicating with clients and HMRC by post, email, telephone and face to face. Tax legislation is not a simple matter, so these communications can be very complex. You need to be able to argue your case clearly, convincingly and diplomatically.

All tax positions have an element of advisory work to them. The advice you give could be on starting a business or on selling property and calculating tax liable on capital gains. You might prepare and explain tax returns, and you will have to get to grips with constantly changing tax laws – this is something you may have to read up on or you might take courses in your own time. While the work is predominantly numerical, there is also a lot of reading and writing involved. In smaller firms, you might have a broader range of responsibilities, whereas in larger organisations you are likely to specialise in one particular aspect of tax.

It is important that you understand that the work is very deadline-based and clients are often slow in providing the necessary information, which can then place you under huge pressure. They may even blame you for any fines incurred! You may also need to record all your work, minute by minute, on a time sheet. You also need to be, and consistently remain, completely up to date with the latest laws and regulations.

Once trained, you could progress in professional practice to partner level, or potentially move internally to a company's tax department. Tax specialisms can be particularly lucrative.

Profile: Tolley® Exam Training

Tolley® Exam Training

Tolley Exam Training is one of the leading national training providers for tax qualifications. Through a combination of highly experienced tutors, quality training material and our unique online services, Tolley Exam Training offers the best study experience available. We consistently achieve exceptional pass rates that significantly surpass the national average – making it the natural choice when enrolling with a training provider in order to pursue a career in taxation.

Tolley Exam Training offers:

- some of the most experienced and well-known tutors in the country

- a proven track record for securing outstanding pass rates

- access to Tolley's Online Academy with study manuals, audio-visual lectures and student and tutor forums, meaning you can study anytime, anywhere

- Tolley's Performance Tracker, enabling you to view your study plan online and download practice exams and answers, allowing you to track your performance

- a free one-year subscription to *Taxation* magazine.

Exceptional pass rates

We consistently achieve outstanding pass rates that significantly surpass the national average and we are confident that we will continue to do so.

ATT May 2012 Examination

Paper	Tolley Exam Training*	National average
Paper 1	97.7%	71.9%
Paper 2	96.8%	72.3%
Paper 3	100.0%	92.2%
Paper 4	100.0%	87.3%
Paper 5	100.0%	81.5%
Paper 6	83.3%	86.8%

*Students who have studied with our Guaranteed Pass Scheme

CTA May 2012 Examination

Paper	Tolley Exam Training* pass rate	National average pass rate
Awareness	98%	86%
Advisory	87%	44%
Application	94%	58%

* Students who have studied with our Guaranteed Pass Scheme

Regional training centres

Due to the successful launch of our five regional training centres, we now offer classroom training at seven locations nationwide:

- Belfast

- Birmingham

- Bristol

- Edinburgh

- London

- Manchester

- Newcastle.

Qualifications offered

We are unique in the training market, being the only organisation that provides training exclusively for professional tax examinations.

We offer training for the following examinations:

- Taxation Technician (ATT) – set by the Association of Taxation Technicians and aimed at those working in tax compliance

- Chartered Tax Adviser (CTA) – set by the Chartered Institute of Taxation and aimed at those wishing to become tax advisers

- ICAS Tax Qualification – set by the Institute of Chartered Accountants of Scotland and aimed at any tax professional working in a compliance or advisory role

- Advanced Diploma in International Taxation (ADIT) – set by the Chartered Institute of Taxation and aimed at those who want to further their careers in international tax

- Associate of the Institute of Indirect Taxation (AIIT) – set by the Institute of Indirect Taxation and aimed at those wishing to become tax advisers in the field of indirect taxation.

- VAT Compliance Diploma (VCD) – set by the Institute of Indirect Taxation and aimed at those wishing to gain an entry-level qualification in, or improve their knowledge of, VAT.

Innovative study system

Guaranteed Pass Scheme – our experience and previous pass rates show us that students who follow the Tolley Exam Training programme have a very high chance of passing the examinations. As a result, we have introduced the Guaranteed Pass Scheme. All students enrolled with us on this programme will be given one free correspondence and revision course in the unlikely event that they fail their examinations.

Tolley's Online Academy allows you to study anytime, anywhere. You will be able to access all of our course manuals and questions banks via the Online Academy. You can view the audio-visual lectures online and download the audio files of the lectures to a media player.

Help is never far away through the use of the tutor and student forums. The forums allow students to access our tutors' words of advice and to help build a study network by making contact with other students in different parts of the country.

The Online Academy is not only making studying more accessible, it is also making it simpler by having everything you need in one place. You can even access the legislation online, by using the links in the online manuals.

Tolley's Performance Tracker allows you full access to view your study programme and track your progress by comparing it with that of your peers.

For more information on Tolley Exam Training, visit www.tolley.co.uk/examtraining, email examtraining@tolley.co.uk or call 020 3364 4500.

Case study

Simon Groom, Director of Tax Training and Professional Development at Tolley, the UK tax division of LexisNexis

All of a sudden tax is front-page news, tax is no longer a boring subject never to be discussed, everyone has an opinion. No one can have missed the controversy around Jimmy Carr and his tax affairs, or the comments about members of Take That and the scheme they are said to have been involved in to reduce their tax bill. The Prime Minister is commenting publicly, and almost every journalist seems to want to have their say. People are divided but no one can deny that tax and accountancy are high profile at the moment, and they look set to stay that way for some time to come.

So what is it all about and why should you consider a career in tax?

The debate is all around tax avoidance. We should establish at this stage that tax avoidance is legal, and there are no suggestions that those whose tax affairs have been discussed in the press were acting illegally in any way. The question being raised is whether the way in which they acted was immoral.

If you were asked if you would like to legitimately reduce the amount of tax you pay, most people would say 'yes', as long as it were legal. Reducing your tax bill is tax avoidance, and therefore if most people would do it, it must be OK. But, for most people, the scope for reducing your tax bill is limited, and you wouldn't want to pay someone a lot of money to advise you how to do it, so most of us don't bother to take advice.

If you are very wealthy, the opportunities for reducing your tax bill are greater, the amounts involved are much bigger, and therefore you might be prepared to pay someone to look at ways of doing it. Surely, in principle, that's just the same as those of us who don't have lots of money, it just happens that the sums involved are bigger?

But now look at it another way. If there are people paying less tax it means that the government has less to spend on public services, or reducing the deficit, and therefore it might decide to raise additional tax elsewhere, by, for example, raising duty on petrol and diesel, meaning the ordinary person pays more.

It's at that point that some people take a different view, and point to the inherent unfairness of it. They would argue that if the wealthy pay less tax, the rest of us pay more. Unfair? Immoral? I'll leave that for you to decide.

Whatever your opinion, there is no question that the government wants to go down the morality route, to try to shame people into not indulging in what they call 'aggressive tax planning'. The problem is, where do you draw the line? One person's aggressive tax planning might seem perfectly reasonable to another.

There is also no doubt that as tax becomes more complicated and the debate continues, the demand for tax advisers will grow.

All of a sudden, tax is sexy!

To find out more about getting the qualifications necessary for a career in tax, visit www.tolley.co.uk/examtraining, call 020 3364 4500 or email examtraining@tolley.co.uk

Corporate finance

As with the areas mentioned previously, you can work in-house or in professional practice in corporate finance. This area is primarily concerned with mergers, demergers, acquisitions and ownership changes. The work may involve the analysis and valuation of target companies and funding of projects to set up, purchase, grow or improve businesses. It may also be necessary to consider and create new equity structures and shareholder bases in stock market flotations, or to restructure debt and related securities. Alternatively, it could involve financing large public sector infrastructure projects. As you can see, it can be one of the most dynamic, creative, strategic and exciting fields, but it is also particularly high pressure and can involve long hours. There can be a lot of contact with other people and negotiation with stakeholders such as funders, bankers, lawyers and analysts.

Corporate finance can involve corporate or private equity transactions and you could be working on either the 'buy' or the 'sell' side of the deal. You could work with the chief financial officer (CFO) and group treasurer on transactions such as:

- mergers and acquisitions

- business disposals

- management buy-outs and buy-ins

- due diligence

- valuations

- raising finance and flotations

- joint ventures and shareholders' agreements

- strategic and exit route planning

- reporting and transaction support.

Responsibilities might include:

- supporting the corporate finance team in the field

- preparing reports, memos, presentations and documents

- preparing financial models in Excel

- providing clients with value-adding recommendations for improvements to processes and controls

- scoping engagements, detailing budgets and time frames

- drafting pitch, proposal and tender documents

- acting as the point of contact in engagements

- liaising and communicating clients' feedback, and identifying and presenting potential solutions to project managers

- assisting in the preparation for and follow-up from senior meetings attended

- general correspondence, administration and billing

- collation and analysis of relevant documentation and information, drafting outputs as directed by the project manager

- producing quality schedules and appendices for reports

- supporting internal and external practice in business development

- supervising and developing junior staff.

It is possible to train in the corporate finance division of a large Public Practice, although smaller firms might start all trainees in audit. It may be more difficult to train on the client side in this specialism as it tends to be a more experienced finance professional, such as the financial director or CFO, who oversees transactions.

You could be assigned to advisory, transaction or reorganisation divisions. On the advisory side, you would be helping the client with what they should do. You would discuss their best course of action, which company to buy and how to raise the finance. In transaction divisions, you would be involved in in-depth financial analysis to decide whether the company is on a sound footing and whether or not it is an entity your client should be considering buying, perhaps at a lower price. In reorganisation, it is likely you would be working with a struggling company trying to organise a turnaround, or, if all else fails, initiating administration proceedings. Reorganisation can be a challenging division to work in, as it can be tough making these types of decisions.

Corporate finance is a varied field. One day you may be meeting a target company's management and finance teams to gather information, and on another day you may be discussing transaction progress on the client's site. Then again, you may spend time in the office checking that there are no conflicts of interest before taking on a particular transaction and performing the in-depth analysis or drawing up the report. On occasion there may even be quieter catch-up days and days for internal and external training. One of the satisfactions is likely to be going into a business and familiarising yourself with all aspects of its working and how it ticks, rather than focusing on just one small element. Within just a matter of days you will know how the company works inside out and how everything fits together.

You need to present yourself well and be strong in relationship-building as there is a lot of liaison involved with different teams of accountants, lawyers and advisory personnel on both sides of the transaction. People can, of course, be a source of frustration in this line of work. You may be reliant on their help and unable to move on with what you are working on because you are waiting for management to send some information or lawyers to forward you documentation. IT literacy is also important, as is numeracy, as there is a lot of financial analysis and daily use of Excel. Do not be afraid to ask lots of questions at first, as you need to be entirely sure of what is being asked of you so you do not have to go back and change everything.

Salaries, including perks and benefits, incentives and rewards can be good, and, while professional, the ethos should not be too stuffy or boring. There is often a good mix of gender, age and character, and the environment can be surprisingly open-plan, fun and chatty. With potentially 50 graduates all starting simultaneously in larger firms, again you can have an instant peer group.

Hours can be long at times, but are typically 9a.m. to 6p.m. You may have to travel, perhaps internationally, depending on where the client and target companies are situated. However, some of the work has to be completed in the office, especially if it involves particularly sensitive or privileged information.

As with all specialisms, you might progress every two to three years to the next level, starting as an associate or trainee and then rising through the ranks of assistant manager and manager, assistant director and director, to partner. Alternatively, you may choose to move into industry, or into banking or a private equity firm. You can move into corporate finance after starting in audit, but by starting in corporate finance you already have three years' valuable experience by the time you qualify.

Business recovery and insolvency

This is a Public Practice field where, as you can imagine, emotions can run high. Ideally, when a company is in financial difficulty, you will be in a position to restructure to improve cashflow, renegotiate existing finances and put the struggling firm back onto a strong footing. However, in certain instances, the company will be deemed insolvent and there will be no possible rescue strategy. As the adviser you will need to sensitively and professionally advise on the legal and practical aspects of winding down, disposing of assets and settling debts with creditors. In such situations there is little room for sentiment and you will need to adopt a hard-headed approach.

Insolvency may be defined as when a company has cashflow difficulties and cannot pay debts as they become due, or when it has a balance sheet deficit between net assets and debts. Therefore the firm may be cashflow-insolvent but balance-sheet-solvent, should it have sufficient illiquid assets. The reverse may also be true, should it have a balance sheet deficit but strong cashflow. Many firms operate in this state without default, due to circumstances such as bank loans and investor funding. To be insolvent, the firm has to be deemed both cashflow and balance-sheet-insolvent.

New legislation encourages restructuring and remodelling of finances to enable the business to continue, but in certain instances liquidation will be the only solution. To give the firm time to restructure and recover, it may be placed in administration, which provides temporary protection from creditors. Voluntary arrangements may then be made with creditors to accept regular monthly payments and perhaps agree to write off part of the debt. As an insolvency specialist, one of your responsibilities would be to manage all this. You would advise clients on how to reorganise corporate entities, realise or dispose of assets, settle creditor claims and distribute any surplus to shareholders.

Each company's situation will be different. As the specialist you may be the first point of contact in engagements, responsible for handling statutory requirements and for writing reports and liaising with creditors regarding progress in the voluntary or compulsory administration process. The work is varied; you may be on site, dealing with customers, suppliers and other stakeholders, or in the office, investigating the directors' conduct in the case of insolvency (directors are not allowed to continue running a firm they know to be in trouble). The business could be of any type and in any industry, such as consumer goods, energy, financial services, real estate, manufacturing, telecommunications, leisure and so on, and there can be many surprises. As we have seen recently, even seemingly well-established firms can quickly collapse in an economic downturn: for example, MFI, Dolphin Bathrooms and Woolworths. However, it is not just retail companies that have been in trouble – Northern Rock and a number of football clubs have also collapsed recently.

Obviously, it is not only businesses that become insolvent, and in certain instances you may be dealing with the bankruptcy of individuals. Again, this calls for great empathy and sensitivity, while maintaining a pragmatic and professional stance.

Forensic accounting

In Public Practice, forensic accounting involves 'detective' investigation in fraud, divorce and personal injury cases. It means logically looking for clues and anomalies in often vast amounts of complex and 'hidden' financial data. You would then have to collate and present your findings, perhaps as an expert witness in court. Extensive accounting and legal knowledge is needed, but it also calls for the understanding of IT systems and skills and sensitivity in interviewing. As a forensic accountant, you might work for law firms, the police, Public Practice firms, banks or government agencies.

However, the work can sometimes feel like a thankless task. In spite of some personal satisfaction in solving the puzzle and proving how it was done and by whom when you uncover a major fraud and loss to a company the organisation can be embarrassed and keen to cover up rather than heralding you as the hero. That said, external stakeholders should appreciate your efforts.

Forensic accountants specialise in the financial models, tools and techniques to gather evidence to globally accepted standards; this will include expertise in the systems and technologies involved in doing this. As the 'detectives' of the financial world, they are often multi-qualified and trained to look for anomalies and hidden clues. As a forensic accountant you might also consider patterns of human behaviour, follow trails left by economic transactions, or search and recover electronic records – whether they are lost by accident or deliberately – to find the true facts or correct financial value.

You would also routinely investigate insurance claims, corporate transactions and civil disputes such as divorce, or criminal disputes including fraud. You would place a value on assets for business funding, operation or liquidation, and delve into public sector losses, fraud and compliance or governance issues.

Financial control

This is an internal operational role primarily concerned with cashflow and efficiency, timeliness of payments to and from the firm, and the day-to-day management of the finance function. You need to be a systematic and organised individual, but have an eye on the bigger picture and the payments that are in the pipeline.

This is often the stepping stone to the role of financial director. It is a senior, pivotal role in a company where you will be involved in all major business decisions and acquisitions and you are likely to have managerial responsibility for the bookkeeping and administrative staff. Indeed, this may be your first experience of people management on a large scale and therefore it is important to foster a climate of mutual respect. You will need to develop softer people skills, as a disciplinarian approach is no longer acceptable. This may not always come naturally to more 'black or white' types, the type of person who may typically be drawn to accounting.

Financial controllers head up financial activities ranging from analysis, to reporting, to more strategic operations. It is a hands-on role as it is concerned with cashflow, accounts production, target-setting, departmental monitoring, auditing and oversight of tax, regulatory and compliance issues. The main aim is to ensure efficiency and best practice.

Your responsibilities might include:

- developing effective systems and procedures

- creating frameworks for financial control, accountability and authority

- developing efficient and secure central accounting systems

- liaising with and informing external auditors

- ensuring adherence to group policies and accounting standards

- providing recommendations for financial improvement or control

- drafting of statutory accounts for the group.

Financial directorship

Financial directors work in-house and take a senior and influential role, adopting the ultimate responsibility for financial strategies and risks. They oversee, change and take responsibility for financial analysis, planning and reporting at senior and board level. As the name suggests, they direct and shape the finance function and impact on the senior decision-making of the company.

Obviously, duties will depend somewhat on the company size and the laws of the country it is in, but as the financial director you would oversee all financial aspects of company strategy and the flow of information to the CEO, board and external stakeholders, such as investors and banks.

You will need to build your own team, whether capitalising on available talent or bringing in new blood. It is common for financial directors to take their closest associate with them when they move jobs as they need to have a safe pair of hands that they can trust to deal with the day-to-day operations. As a financial director, you need to be relieved of the hands-on responsibility so that you can concentrate on the broader picture and wider strategy.

Your responsibilities generally include:

- overall control of a business's financial strategy

- planning, managing, evaluating and reporting on a number of issues including the development of policies, systems and processes

- compliance-consistent reporting and accounting, including taxation, dividends, and the annual report and accounts

- analysing sales projections and income against actual figures and suggesting improvements to the planning process

- assessing long-term financial trends and reviewing prospects for future growth of income and new product areas, in conjunction with the board

- oversight of financial communications strategy, for example for the stock market, business press and business analysts' community

- recruitment, selection, training, motivation and management of financial personnel

- strategic planning and development with the executive team, recording and disseminating information and reports to executive and management teams

- in some cases dealing with company insurance, import/export administration, licensing, legal areas and activities, corporate-level negotiations (e.g. regarding premises, plant, trading, acquisitions and divestments, disposals), contracts and agreements, major supplier/customer/partner relationships, regulatory body relationships, approvals and accreditations

- some IT responsibilities

- some environmental/sustainability and CSR responsibilities

- some quality assurance or health and safety responsibilities

- company secretary/corporate finance responsibilities should there
  not be an appointed company secretary or treasurer – this work
  includes the statutory company and capital requirements, debt,
  equity, and mergers and acquisitions administration

- company director responsibilities, if appropriate.

Management accounting

Most management accountants work in-house, but there can be opportunities in the advisory divisions of Public Practice. Management accounting involves taking a broader perspective on the business and liaising with different business functions on resourcing issues. As a management accountant, you would generate regular internal reports that would enable the managers to monitor performance and forecast and plan appropriately. You might also advise on the financial implications of projects, explain the financial consequences of earlier decisions made, and monitor and control finances, as well as conduct internal audits and devise strategies in light of the competitive landscape in which you are working.

The role of the management accountant is increasingly as a business partner to the line managers, ensuring that they have accurate, timely and relevant information to aid their decision-making and planning. You would act as a change agent by evaluating existing measures and procedures and then making recommendations for improvements.

Your typical responsibilities might be:

- managing a team in the production of management accounts

- advising and supporting senior executives and directors and producing
  weekly, monthly and quarterly management reports for them

- evaluating productivity models, analysing budget variances and
  exploring potential problems with line managers: because of this it

is important to build strong and positive working relationships with departmental heads as you will need these people on your side for you to be successful in your work

- developing and revising strategic plans and recommendations for business improvement and innovation

- preparing tax returns, statements of cashflow and income and expenditure accounts

- appraising and improving financial information systems informing budgets, forecasts and business planning

- controlling financial expenditure and establishing and maintaining costing models

- project planning and resourcing and pre-empting potential problems or opportunities

- any ad hoc research and analysis, providing commentary and conclusions

- helping the company to comply with industry regulations.

Unlike in financial accounting, management accounting is less concerned with retrospective, historic data and more concerned with the future. It is focused on the 'big picture' and timeliness is arguably more important than the pinpoint accuracy of audited financial statements, which is evidenced by the fact that management accountants are not qualified to audit in Public Practice. As a management accountant, you would not be confined by traditional accounting practices, but you would have the opportunity to delve into operational research and other economic and statistical models. You might focus more on individual aspects of the business and on areas such as market, product and sales trends. It could be exciting if you like to think quickly on your feet and to find innovative solutions, but a perfectionist may find management accountancy too imprecise and unpredictable.

Financial analysis

In both internal and practice roles, financial analysis can be quite quantitative. The reason for this is that you are looking for evidence of whether something is working or not, or whether or not it would be a viable proposition. This role can be varied as often the projects you would be working on are bespoke, but there may also be routine reporting as well. Financial analysts work in all industries including retail, FMCGs, property, banking and financial services, software, telecommunications, oil and entertainment.

Financial analysis involves delving into the detail of what is really happening financially. You need to collate and analyse data, identify trends and make recommendations for significant changes that will aim to optimise pricing and processes, minimise costs and waste, and produce measurable benefits. As the analyst, you may be the main interface between the finance department and other divisions within the company. At junior level, the hard analysis and factual research and verification will be your responsibility, whereas planning and decision-making on the basis of those findings will be the job of more senior financial analysts.

Typical responsibilities would include:

- analysis of reports from sales, marketing, purchasing, production and communication divisions, using statistical software and spreadsheets, producing your own reports and making recommendations for continuous improvement

- undertaking research, identifying trends, risks and opportunities, variance and anomalies, and performing peer or competitor analysis to formulate accurate forecasts

- keeping up to date with and developing new tools, models, indicators and techniques for financial planning and forecasting

- reporting on organic changes, challenging assumptions and liaising with senior decision-makers to evaluate and monitor the impact of planned interventions and changes that are devised to improve efficiency and measurable performance

- in a financial institution, extracting information to gain insight into a company's prospects and managerial effectiveness and advising on any investment decisions.

Financial analysis work can be varied and stimulating. By reading between the lines and conducting your own research, quantitative analysis and modelling, you can unearth some interesting and useful information about the realities of the company's, peer's or competitor's financial situation, including their functioning and direction. It provides scope for detective work, creativity, fact-finding and generating innovative and practical solutions and recommendations, both strategic and operational.

Financial analysis can be both retrospective and forward-thinking. It is not always focused on spreadsheets and balance sheets, and the project work provides variety and a clear goal. However, financial analysis may be frustrating in that ultimately you are not in control or making the decisions yourself. It will be up to someone else whether they choose to listen to and act on your advice, actually implementing your recommendations or simply leaving your hard work in a filing cabinet where it will be forgotten!

2

The professional bodies

The key professional bodies and qualifications

The qualification and route into accountancy that you choose should be a matter of personal preference and circumstances, so it helps to consider why accountancy appeals to you in the first place.

- Is there something specific that has drawn you to this profession?

- Is there a particular financial specialism that has attracted you and, if so, why?

- In what sort of company or sector could you see yourself working?

- Where can you see your career going in the longer term?

It is imperative that you carefully research the options available for study, the syllabuses and emphases of different qualifications, the types of accountancy firms and settings, and their different ethos, requirements and opportunities.

You also need to carry out some self-analysis and identify your motivations, abilities and personal qualities. It can be helpful to talk to someone who knows you well about the areas of accountancy and discuss between you which of them would suit you best. Equally, you could seek more objective advice from a professional career consultant who may have psychometric tools to help inform your decision. Such considerations and the resulting self-awareness, clarity and focus should ensure that you make the right choices and serve you well in selection interviews.

What are the primary professional qualifications and what is the difference between them? The answer is that there are four main examining bodies, and each one is different to the others. These will all be discussed in detail in this chapter. The four bodies are:

1. ICAEW (Institute of Chartered Accountants in England and Wales), along with its Scottish (ICAS) and Irish (ICAI) equivalents

2. ACCA (Association of Chartered Certified Accountants)

3. CIMA (Chartered Institute of Management Accountants)

4. CIPFA (Chartered Institute of Public Finance and Accountancy).

There is also the AAT (Association of Accounting Technicians), which has its own stand-alone award; this is often used as a foundation qualification for the professional qualifications offered by the other professional bodies. This will be discussed further in Chapter 5.

The Professional Overright Board's (POB's) 2012 survey report, *Key Facts and Trends in the Accountancy Profession*, groups the 312,000 qualified accountants in the UK, and 438,000 globally, by qualifying body. It also provides sector and gender percentages. Table 4 shows the breakdown.

TABLE 4: Members of professional accountancy bodies

	UK members	Worldwide members	In practice (%)	In industry and commerce (%)	In the public sector (%)	Women (%)
ACCA	75,305	151,283	26	56	10	44
CIMA	69,038	87,316	2	72	16	32
CIPFA	13,159	13,544	3	8	62	31
ICAEW	117,475	138,464	31	42	3	25
ICAI	18,814	20,905	29	57	4	37
ICAS	16,666	19,334	28	42	3	31
AIA*	1,647	7,300	5	84	1	29

Source: POB, *Key Facts and Trends in the Accountancy Profession*, June 2012
* Association of International Accountants

Trainee representation of different professional bodies in Public Practice, January 2012

Accountancy magazine's annual survey of the top 60 firms' trainees found that in January 2012 there were 12,137 students training under the five major professional bodies, compared with 11,642 in January 2011. There were 8,070 ICAEW trainees (66.5%), 2,085 ICAS trainees (17%), 1,173 ACCA students (10%), 784 CIMA students (6.5%) and 61 trainees taking the CIPFA qualification (0.5%).

The Big Four account for 73% of all students. The proportions for the Big Four are: 66.5% ICAEW, 20% ICAS, 6% ACCA, 8% CIMA and 0.5% CIPFA. Of the top 60 firms in the survey 84% of trainees are ICAEW and ICAS students, which means that the vast majority in the top 60 Public Practice firms are ACA/ACCA (chartered accountancy) trainees.

While the ICAEW maintains its position as having the largest number of UK members, ACCA and CIMA numbers have remained steady over the last five years, and the ACCA has a good representation globally.

CIMA and CIPFA have the lowest percentage of trainees in professional practice: 2% and 3% respectively, compared with approximately one-third of all ICAEW members, including non-working members or those working in 'other' fields such as a professional body. However, CIMA has the highest proportion of members working in industry and commerce (nearly three-quarters), and CIPFA is well represented in the public sector (nearly two-thirds). The figures in Table 4 do not total 100% because some members are retired, currently unemployed, or working in none of the listed sectors.

Popularity by gender

Proportionally, ACCA has the highest percentage of women members (44%), compared with just 25% who are ICAEW members. CIMA has seen a large increase in female members in recent years, with approximately a third of its qualified members being female, as well as having around 44% female students.

ACCA has always encouraged women, which can be seen by it being the first professional body to welcome a female member, Ethel Ayres Purdie in 1909; she was also one of the first female accountants.

In 1971, Vera di Palma made history as the first ACCA council member and then in 1980 as the first female president. ACCA scored another first when Anthea Rose became ACCA's first chief executive, and indeed the first of any professional accountancy body in the world, holding the position for a decade.

In 2007, after a period as finance director with the University of Birmingham, Gill Ball was elected president of the ACCA council by other members. However, she was still only the third female to hold this position, as for the other 26 years ACCA had a male president. Helen Brand has been CEO since 2008 and she acknowledges that ACCA challenges the establishment and focuses on talent and ambition, making it inspiring and meritocratic. Brand believes that the ACCA culture of customer service and the role of accountants in creating and managing the economic upturn (in due course) will provide excellent prospects for accountants, an increasing number of whom will be women.

Institute of Chartered Accountants in England and Wales: ICAEW (ACA)

The ICAEW (www.icaew.com) was established by Royal Charter in 1880 and has in excess of 138,000 members worldwide and over 117,000 in the UK. The ICAEW represents chartered accountants and oversees the ACA qualification.

ACA is perceived as the most prestigious and competitive of the accountancy qualifications and it has been reported that the majority of financial directors in FTSE companies are ACA-qualified, many through the Big Four firms. It is a rigorous and sought-after qualification in business as well as in banking and finance. This is because chartered accountants act as business advisers too. They aim to maximise profitability and to inform high-level strategic decisions that will increase market share for client companies. They undertake audits and provide financial reports and information, and may specialise in insolvency, audit, taxation, corporate finance, treasury, forensic accounting or accounting systems. The majority of training opportunities are in Public Practice, but there are increasing opportunities in industry. After qualifying, they may choose to work in-house, in any industrial, corporate, public or not-for-profit sector.

Typically, chartered accountants spend time liaising with clients and providing financial information and advice. This includes reviewing company systems and performing checks to analyse risk. They advise on transactions such as mergers and acquisitions, insolvency, tax and fraud, besides managing colleagues. In internal roles they liaise with internal and external auditors and from these meetings they produce reports and recommendations as well as preparing statements, financial reports and accounts. They may take responsibility for planning and forecasting, and also perhaps for negotiating with suppliers and creditors.

The ICAEW promotes chartered accountancy as affording great variety, challenge, excitement and security as well as it being an excellent route to a very rewarding career in business leadership. As you will be learning while earning, you will be highly marketable, plus there's the bonus of a good income; your salary should double on qualification. ACA has the highest pass rate but this does

FIGURE 1: Main accountancy bodies

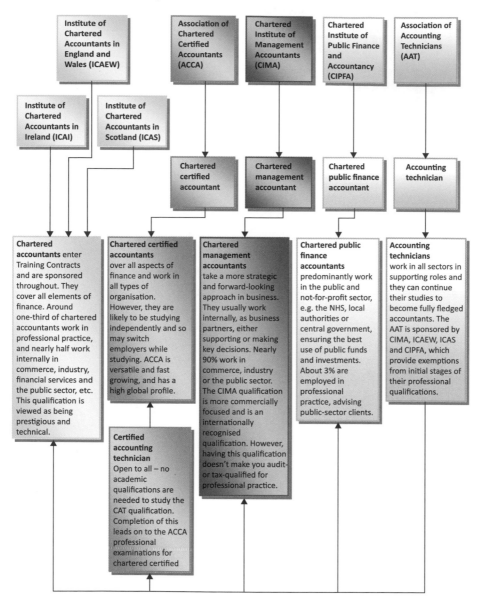

not necessarily mean it has the easiest examinations. Its success rate may reflect the calibre of students and the level of support afforded to trainees. Undoubtedly the ACA qualification provides credibility and marketability for the most senior positions, as more CEOs, CFOs and chairpersons are qualified in ACA than any other professional qualification. Career choices on qualification are endless. The POB survey published in 2012 found 31% of members to be in Public Practice.

ACA is a two-stage qualification. You will be earning well, but study on top of a full workload can be very demanding. In the initial Professional Stage you study six knowledge modules that cover core competencies which underpin accountancy, as well as six further modules with a more applied, practical element; these involve work experience, advising and problem-solving in various scenarios. The subsequent Advanced Stage involves two more complex technical papers covering business reporting and business change as well as a case study. ACA is often purported to be intellectually demanding – more so than other professional qualifications – and you are committed to the employer to whom you are contracted, so you cannot change employer mid-studies.

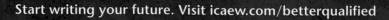

I AM THE FUTURE CEO OF...

THE CHARTERED ACCOUNTANT. NO ONE'S BETTER QUALIFIED.

Ambition's a funny thing. Simply having it isn't enough; knowing what to do with it really makes the difference. That's why no one trains to be an ICAEW Chartered Accountant by accident. And it's certainly no accident 84% of FTSE 100 companies have an ICAEW Chartered Accountant on their board. How far will your ambition take you?

Start writing your future. Visit icaew.com/betterqualified

ICAEW

Profile: ICAEW

Opportunity, variety and the ability to work in any industry, anywhere in the world, are just some of the benefits of becoming an ICAEW chartered accountant.

Whether it's giving business advice to a high-street retail chain, testifying as an expert witness in court or ensuring the business sustainability of a multinational corporation, chartered accountants are vital to the success of any organisation.

Being 'chartered' means you are recognised as being at the top of your profession. It shows you have developed industry-specific skills and experience, not just academic and theoretical knowledge.

The ACA qualification from ICAEW gives you the skills and expertise the business world demands. Your ACA training ensures you have a solid foundation in business, accounting and finance, which you can transfer and apply throughout your career to any sector of business, anywhere in the world.

Your route to success

You can start the ACA at a number of stages in your education; as a school leaver, after a qualification such as the AAT or ICAEW's Certificate in Finance, Accounting and Business, or as a graduate.

ICAEW also has a number of partnership programmes with universities and employers to help you get the most from your time at university. Experience gained on internships and placements can be recognised and you can also gain credit towards some ACA modules depending on the degree course you study.

To ensure you get the best experience and to qualify as an ICAEW chartered accountant, you will need to secure a training agreement with an ICAEW-authorised employer. Training agreements vary depending on the route you choose but will typically last between three and five years. Your employer is committed to your ACA training and will give you all the practical experience and exam support you need. You are supported throughout your training by ICAEW, with access to online material, support sessions, webinars and career help and advice.

The combined commitment from your employer, ICAEW and you to your ACA training ensures that upon qualifying as an ICAEW chartered accountant you can demonstrate you have the skills and expertise to be valuable to any organisation, whichever sector they are in.

To find out more about how to become an ICAEW chartered accountant, visit icaew.com/careers

Case study

Rachael, BrightStart student, Deloitte LLP

One of the things that put me off going to university was the debt I would have accrued. I liked the idea of earning while I learned!

I initially considered a career in textiles; however, while studying for my A levels I realised my focus shifted and that it wasn't the creative side of textiles I was interested in, but the business side.

Despite being offered a place at the University of Southampton I decided to take a gap year, which is when Deloitte's BrightStart programme caught my eye. Following my application, various tests, interviews and an assessment day, I was selected to become part of the first-ever BrightStart intake in September 2011.

I would recommend a programme like this to anyone who is looking for an alternative route into chartered accountancy and the ACA qualification, and who doesn't necessarily want to go to university.

James, Francis Clark, Exeter

I studied Pharmacy at the University of Bath but after realising that a career as a pharmacist wasn't for me I started to look at alternative career options. I had always been interested in business and finance and a summer with the *Financial Times* confirmed my motivation to work within the finance industry. I searched the ICAEW careers website and got in contact with accounting firms I thought would provide a broad range of experience combined with the opportunity to take on responsibility early on in my career.

I enjoy the variation of working across different industries with different people and processes. I have now begun taking on senior jobs on site, so as well as calculating expectations, reconciling figures, preparing schedules and discussing matters with the client and the team, I am also focusing on the higher-risk areas of the file, delegating work and supporting other team members.

My job isn't all about numbers, accountancy is a much broader look at business and finance, and investing three years in gaining experience and a valuable qualification is well worth it!

Scotland and Ireland

The relevant body for chartered accountancy qualifications in Scotland is the **Institute of Chartered Accountants of Scotland** (www.icas.org.uk).

The ICAS works with 19,000 business professionals across 100 countries and has 3,000 students studying its professional qualification to become a qualified chartered accountant.

It is also possible to study for this Scottish qualification in the rest of the UK. For example, Ernst & Young favours ICAS; according to *Accountancy's* top 60 trainee survey, 54% of its trainees are studying for the ICAS qualification. This may be because examinations are 'front-loaded' — you cram at college early on to accelerate a strong technical foundation.

Founded by Royal Charter in 1854, the ICAS is the original accountancy body and it pioneered the International Accounting Standards. It is one of the fastest-growing accountancy bodies, with the number of students starting training contracts increasing substantially over the last couple of years. ICAS both trains and examines, which leads to the high standards that are substantiated by the positive assessments it receives from the POB. Only ICAS members can use the label CA (chartered accountant), as others use the designation ACA.

The relevant body for chartered accountancy in Ireland is the **Institute of Chartered Accountants in Ireland** (www.charteredaccountants.ie).

With over 20,000 members and around 5,750 students, the ICAI is the leading voice for chartered accountancy in both the Republic of Ireland and Northern Ireland. Established by Royal Charter in 1888, ICAI is the largest and longest-established accountancy body in Ireland, with members being bound by its handbook of rules regarding professionalism and ethics.

The ICAI is represented in over 90 countries with the majority of members working internally in finance, business and industry and the remainder working in professional practice advising a wide variety of clients.

What are the ACA entry requirements?

It is possible to enter chartered accountancy as a school leaver with A levels or an AAT qualification, but in reality 80% of trainees are graduates. Indeed, many training employers will not only demand at least 2.i honours but also a UCAS tariff above 260, and you are likely to be put through a rigorous selection procedure involving psychometric tests, role-plays and interviews. Smaller firms may accept an applicant with 2.ii honours, but nearly 90% of graduate ACA trainees have a First or 2.i honours. Entry requirements may change depending on the country you study in, so you will need to check the local requirements.

Does it matter what degree you have?

No it doesn't! An A level in Maths is not a prerequisite; nor is a business, accounting, economics or finance degree. So whatever degree discipline you have studied or are looking to study, accountancy could be an option. However, evidence of commercial understanding and relevant work experience will be viewed favourably and is very important if you want to be a success.

The graduate ACA intake largely has business or finance degrees, and science, mathematics and engineering qualifications are also popular, but this may be more to do with self-selection than any recruitment bias. Accountancy appeals to facts- and figures-orientated people. Should your degree be in a relevant subject, you may be able to gain credits towards professional qualifications.

Being a graduate isn't the only route to gaining an ACA qualification: you can study for the qualification upon leaving school. For entry after your A levels, the minimum requirements are set at three GCSEs in any subjects at grades A*–C, but some employers will stipulate GCSEs in English and Maths as well as two A levels. However, you don't have to have maths, accountancy or business-related subjects. For graduate-level entry, it is important to keep in mind that employers will require 260 UCAS tariff points as a minimum, but others may ask for 300-plus and they will not accept points gained from an A level in General Studies.

The AAT-ACA fast track, otherwise known as the accountancy apprenticeship, affords credits towards professional qualifications. This means that from A level to ACA it can take you just four years; however 77% of AAT-ACA students complete ACA training in three years.

Other skills needed

As well as a genuine interest in finance and technical, sector-specific skills, firms will also be looking for evidence of more general transferable skills. These include:

- business awareness

- self-discipline, motivation and commitment (to combine the demands of work and study)

- analytical and problem-solving skills

- people and communication skills, including report writing

- integrity and trustworthiness

- numeracy skills

- IT literacy

- organisational and time management skills

- initiative and independence

- team-working and networking skills

- management and leadership potential

- flexibility, confidence and drive.

Possible career progression

Within the first three years of training to become an ACA, you will gain more experience and responsibility with the training employer to whom you are contracted. You may take on more client-facing and supervisory duties, and with smaller firms you may be dealing with clients from an earlier stage.

Post-qualification, the opportunities greatly increase. You could stay in professional practice, perhaps transferring to different specialisms, taking secondments abroad and broadening your experience, or simply move up the management ladder with a view to becoming a senior manager after about five years, and eventually a partner within eight to 15 years. You might join a smaller or larger firm, or even go self-employed in the longer term. Your number of options is vast.

Many chartered accountants make a move in-house; according to POB figures, about half work internally in the banking, industry, commercial, public or voluntary sectors. Typically, you would start in internal audit, financial accounting or business analysis immediately after qualifying, although more managerial roles open up with longer experience. It is possible to make finance director within 10 to 15 years, although, due to their comprehensive business training, many chartered accountants eventually take broader general management, chairman and CEO roles.

The working environment

The working environment is formal and you will be expected to wear a suit and to maintain a professional image, at least when client-facing. However, some firms will allow you to dress down when in the office. But it is very important to ensure that you do not allow the formality to stifle your own personality; clients really hate having to deal with a 'dull' auditor!

You are likely to be contracted to work overtime on demand, particularly from January to March, the busiest period for audit. Indeed, hours may be extremely long during these months, especially when working for financial services clients in the City. You do need to do this overtime and to demonstrate a positive attitude towards it; the quickest way to lose the support of your managers and peers is by not contributing to the team effort. You will need to learn how to control your work–life balance for the sake of your sanity.

Your work can also include substantial travel to clients' premises. All your expenses will be reimbursed, and London-based auditors working in financial services may well stay in hotels around the country for many weeks at a time, returning home only at weekends. If you are interested in international travel, it is advisable to apply to firms with overseas offices as you may be seconded to them.

Typical salaries and benefits

Starting salaries vary greatly according to the size and location of the firm, as well as the sector. As you might expect, pay tends to be higher in London and the south east.

According to the ICAEW, typical graduate starting salaries range from £14,500 to £25,500. Figures from the Career Benchmarking Survey 2011 on the ICAEW site show that, in the first two years as an ACA, you might earn on average £45,000 per year. This will increase and can reach over £87,500 for those qualified for nine or more years. However, the average ACA's salary is £82,400 in business, but ACAs working in banking can reach considerably more, with the average being £106,500.

ACAs working in London earn an average basic salary of £92,500, approximately £7,000 more than in other southern regions and about £20,000 to £30,000 more than in northern counties. This is partly due to the higher representation in London of the higher-paid sectors, such as banking, capital markets and insurance.

There are a number of additional benefits, the main one being bonuses. These can average from anything around £1,000 in the early years to as much as £23,000 after 10 to 20 years. Other benefits include a company pension, healthcare, life assurance, car allowances and share options, and can also include leisure facilities, optional holidays, career development, sabbaticals, study support and flexitime. Larger firms often give you a personal 'benefits budget', which you can use to 'purchase' your preferred options, such as extra holiday, coaching or childcare vouchers, or simply a cash pay-out on top of your salary. Additionally, while studying, study support and a 'no overtime' agreement may be available.

Association of Chartered Certified Accountants (ACCA)

The Association of Chartered Certified Accountants (www.accaglobal.com) is the largest and perhaps fastest-growing global accountancy professional body. It has 424,000 students and over 151,000 members in 170 countries.

The Big Four offer the ACCA qualification stream as well, as it affords greater flexibility than ACA. This is due to the fact that you might work for any finance department while studying and, should you wish to, you can even switch jobs and employers. Many trainees train with one of the 8,500 ACCA-approved employers around the world, but this is not essential. The ACCA offers an internationally recognised qualification as it is a global body, rather than UK-based, that focuses on 'professional values, ethics and governance'. ACCA also purports to understand the real issues facing small businesses and this is reflected in the fact that 63,000 of its members work in small and medium-sized enterprises (SMEs) or small partnerships worldwide. High-street accountants who deal with the public are often ACCA-qualified.

On the whole, competition is very fierce, especially in large financial 'blue chip' companies and for industry positions offering good packages for study, so early application in your final degree year is advised.

ACCA accountants develop and maintain financial and accounting systems and records and provide financial forecasts, as well as auditing and investigating any irregularities. They focus on maximising profitability and efficiency whether working internally or for a client organisation, and they may choose to specialise in, for example, insolvency, tax or corporate finance. Pressure can be particularly high at financial year, quarter and month ends. Many large corporations have to submit quarterly updates to their brokers in order to ensure that the financial markets are informed about the firm's progress. ACCA accountants are found in all sectors – public, commercial, industrial and financial services – as well as in professional practice.

The ACCA qualification has 14 examinations and these all need to be passed within 10 years of registering and becoming an ACCA student. There is no time limit, however, for gaining the required three years' practical work experience, although all accountancy studies are easier if you are actually performing relevant work while studying and therefore putting theory into practice. As part of the practical experience requirements, 13 performance objectives need to be monitored and met by an appointed workplace mentor, but this could be before, during or after your studies. The technical areas covered by both ACA and ACCA exams are said to be similar. ACA perhaps places more emphasis on case studies and analysis at the final stage.

So what are the advantages of ACCA? ACCA is a global qualification based on international accounting standards, but can also be tailored to incorporate and test knowledge of legal and tax regulations in your own country. ACCA is perhaps less technically specific and is relevant and applicable to all sectors, whether professional practice or finance departments in the corporate or public sector. As the only professional body with a mandatory ethics module, ACCA has recognised the increasing concern for professionalism and CSR in today's world. Additionally, the flexible approach to continuing professional development (CPD) ensures that development and continuous learning is personally relevant and of practical value, as well as suited to your lifestyle and active involvements, as it gives the opportunity for classroom and conference courses, on-the-job learning and committee membership.

Finally, and uniquely to ACCA, the two final modules enable you as the student to choose the specialist papers most relevant to your career aspirations; these can include advanced financial management, performance management, taxation, audit and assurance.

What are the ACCA entry requirements?

Is a degree essential?

Officially, no degree or HND (BTEC Higher National Diploma) is essential; there are a number of different entry points to the qualification.

With the graduate entry-level route, you may enter from any discipline. The following degree subjects are viewed favourably but they're not essential:

- accountancy and finance

- business and management

- economics

- international business

- mathematics.

A 2.i honours degree is usually required, together with strong A levels and English and Mathematics GCSEs. As an ACCA graduate trainee, if you have a relevant degree from an ACCA-accredited university then you may be exempt from up to nine exams at the fundamental level of the qualification. Even if your qualification is not ACCA-accredited, you may be able to gain exemptions. The ACCA website has an exemption database, so you can see if you qualify.

The ACCA qualification is open to everyone. For school-leaver registration, you must be over 18 years old, with two A levels and three GCSEs in five distinct subjects that must include English and mathematics. If you do not meet these entry requirements, you will need to undertake the Foundations in Accountancy course.

Other skills needed

There are personal motivations, traits and skills required alongside the educational requirements. These include:

- commercial understanding and a general business interest

- self-discipline, motivation and commitment (to combine the demands of work and study)

- analytical skills with a logical approach to work

- problem-solving skills

- interpersonal and communication skills (including written and verbal skills)

- integrity and trustworthiness

- numeracy skills

- IT literacy

- organisational and time management skills

- attention to detail

- initiative, proactivity and independence

- team-working skills with leadership potential.

Increasingly, employers are looking for candidates to have relevant experience, whether from work shadowing, temping, internships or holiday jobs. In today's competitive market you need strong and solid evidence that you want to do, and can do, the work, and that you will fit in.

Possible career progression

The practical element of training ensures both breadth and depth of experience, and once you are ACCA-qualified you might progress further by taking on greater supervisory responsibility and more complex and prestigious clients and projects. You can be awarded a lot of responsibility at an early stage, which can develop from performing operational financial tasks to taking a more strategic role. This can be dependent on individual preferences and ambitions. The broad ACCA syllabus and strategic emphasis also equip you for a wider commercial role and you might subsequently move into general or operational management, or even strategic and consultancy positions.

Alternatively, you may choose to specialise; you can do this in audit, risk or forensic accounting. There is an expectation that you will actively ensure that your knowledge and skill set remain current and in tune with business needs.

In Private Practice, you might expect to reach partner level within 10 years, or you might obtain a practising certificate of your own and set up your own practice or maybe work as a sole trader.

The working environment

Around half of ACCA members work in the corporate sector, with the majority of the rest working in professional, Public Practice and public sector areas. You might work anywhere in the world, because the qualification is offered and recognised in more than 170 countries.

Companies of all sizes, in all industries and every sector train and employ ACCA members. So you can work in any organisation, ranging from aerospace to a charity. Settings are typically formal in major national and international companies and in client-facing Public Practice roles, but smaller companies may accept smart casual attire and suits may not always be obligatory.

Chartered certified accountants generally work a normal 35- to 40-hour week, but you may need to work longer hours or at weekends during peak times or to meet a particular client's pressing needs. Travel to clients' premises may be required, especially in audit, so it could necessitate significant periods away from home. International secondments are also often available in multinational companies. It is suggested that just over a third of ACCA members are afforded flexible working arrangements, with nearly a quarter able to work from home.

Typical salaries and benefits

As with other fields of accountancy, starting salaries vary greatly, again according to size, type and sector of the firm and the qualification you are studying or have studied. Starting salaries can range from £15,000 to £25,000, rising to £30,000 to £52,000 after qualification. At a more senior level, for example 10 years after qualifying, you could command anything up to around £100,000.

Your other benefits might include pension, health insurance, profit share, a car allowance and a bonus.

Chartered Institute of Management Accountants (CIMA)

Management accountants work in organisations of all sizes and in all sectors, and have 195,000 students and members in 176 countries. They are well represented in a number of sectors, including manufacturing, service industries, commerce and industry, the public sector and not-for-profit organisations. People often view accountancy in terms of auditing, but management accountants are much more involved with the day-to-day running and decision-making of an organisation. As the name suggests, they focus on the management of accounting. Management accountants are big picture 'doers', not number-crunching theorists. High-street accountants who work with the public as well as those offering business forecasting and planning in larger Public Practices may be CIMA-qualified (www.cimaglobal.com).

Whereas financial accountants follow GAAP, management accountants select their approaches and techniques from various academic and commercial sources, providing greater freedom and scope for creativity. The CIMA syllabus does not cover external auditing so CIMA members are not able to work in Public Practice and undertake audit projects, but they can work in advisory and consultancy divisions. In order to work in auditing CIMA members would need to cross-qualify with ACA or ACCA, which would require several years' practical audit experience plus additional qualifications.

As a CIMA-qualified 'financial business partner', you would analyse costs, profitability and performance, and prepare budgets across the organisation. You would have a central role in understanding, advising, planning and forecasting on key commercial strategies and in managing risks. You would look to the future and take a predictive rather than retrospective approach, unlike in auditing. Again, you could face particular pressure at financial year and month ends. Additionally, you may negotiate with corporate financiers and communicate financial information to managers in other functions. You may monitor and evaluate financial information systems and internal controls, and design reward structures for shareholders and senior executives.

Why choose CIMA? It is a well-respected and internationally recognised qualification that is specifically tailored for working in business and you may progress to a high-paid, prestigious position.

CIMA's commercial emphasis is particularly apparent when you look at syllabuses for other professional bodies. The different syllabuses reflect the different objectives of the qualifications. Compared with ACCA, CIMA uniquely covers operations, change management, marketing, and relationship and project management. There is also a greater emphasis on HR management and techniques of applied management accounting. Unlike CIMA, ACCA covers taxation, external audit, assurance and law and focuses on information systems in a very different way. So, you can see that ACCA and CIMA qualifications differ greatly.

By definition, the CIPFA syllabus is tailored towards the public sector and does not incorporate CIMA's operational management, marketing, business economics and law, or strategic management modules, but it is unique in covering public-sector-specific accounting issues, external audit and taxation. It also places a different emphasis on audit and assurance, and public finance and policy.

CIMA combines professional examinations and three years' relevant practical experience, which is gained with an employer who can provide appropriate experience or a formal training scheme, although in some cases even university work experience can count. It is sensible to look for good study leave packages because study can be very hard when you are also taking such responsibility within the workplace. The syllabus is revised every four years through consultation to reflect the needs of global business; it was last revised in 2010. In addition to the fundamentals of accounting, CIMA covers strategic business and management skills including:

- analysis to inform business decisions

- strategy to generate wealth and shareholder value

- risk identification and management

- planning and budgeting

- communication and the identification of information needs and dissemination of audience-specific messages.

There are three learning pillars to the 2010 CIMA qualification – enterprise, performance and financial – each with three levels of examinations (operational, management and strategic). The final professional competence level consists of T4, a test of professional competence in management accounting. This level is split into two parts: part A is a work-based practical experience and part B is a case study exam based on both previewed and unseen materials. To achieve chartered status and become an Associate Chartered Management Accountant (ACMA), all levels must be passed. There are no time restrictions.

What are the CIMA entry requirements?

Is a degree required?

CIMA is for everyone, and there are no formal academic requirements. All you need is a genuine interest in business, the drive to succeed and competence in mathematics and English language. Those in this position first complete the entry-level Certificate in Business Accounting. However, exemptions gained through a relevant degree or business experience can speed your progress. A qualification such as a degree in accounting, economics, business, finance, law or even science, the Open University Certificate in Accounting, or an AAT qualification may exempt you from the CIMA certificate stage. You might then go straight to the Professional Qualification level. Otherwise, the Certificate in Business Accounting must be passed before moving on to the CIMA Professional Qualification.

Again, for graduate entry, most employers tend to insist on a 2.i honours degree and a high UCAS tariff, plus strong English and mathematics. Some even specify particular degree subjects. CIMA accepts BTEC HNDs, but employers may not be as flexible. You may have a greater chance with SMEs if you have only a BTEC diploma.

As with the ACA and ACCA, relevant work experience will be viewed favourably and is becoming increasingly important in the face of strong competition. It is also possible to work as a management accountant if you have qualified with one of the other professional bodies.

Profile: Kaplan Financial

KAPLAN
FINANCIAL

Over the last 70 years, Kaplan has become one of the world's largest providers of diversified education, helping individuals like you to achieve your goals and realise your potential. We have over 30,000 employees in over 30 countries delivering courses to more than one million students annually.

We offer a comprehensive portfolio of market-leading training courses for professional accountancy and tax qualifications that develop your industry knowledge and technical expertise as well as key personal and leadership skills required within business.

Kaplan Financial has the combination of award-winning expert tutors, training courses and dedicated support staff to ensure your exam success. Our courses include ACCA, CIMA, AAT and ACA (ICAEW) and are offered in a variety of locations throughout the UK as well as through home study options and online learning. So whether you are a school leaver or a university graduate, we can help you realise your potential.

Contact us to find out more about our range of courses today.

Kaplan Financial: A learning experience as individual as you are

Visit: http://www.kaplanfinancial.co.uk

Email: enquires@kaplanfinancial.co.uk

Call: 0845 873 6314

Case study

James Breen, Kaplan Financial student

James won the 'First in World' prize for the CIMA Enterprise Operations paper.* He studied via Kaplan's Live Online course, which is similar to a classroom course with lectures following a set timetable, but is delivered 100% online.

After graduating from the University of Sheffield in Accounting and Financial Management, James decided to study with Kaplan and never looked back. Read what James said about his experiences since choosing Kaplan:

Why did you choose to study with Kaplan?
From the research I had conducted it was offering the best service within the market for live online learning. Furthermore, Kaplan was offering tutors who had years of experience in both teaching and the financial sector.

What are your thoughts on Kaplan Financial?
Kaplan is an accomplished tuition provider offering a highly structured, effective and professional service. Both the lectures themselves and the study materials provided are clear, concise and provide everything necessary in order to succeed.

I would definitely recommend Kaplan as the three courses I have taken with the company so far have led to outstanding success.

How helpful did you find the resources and materials available to you?
The resources and materials were extremely helpful. The course materials covered the entire syllabus in a concise and detailed manner. In addition, the revision materials provided were key to my success as they gave me hours of exam practice.

Also, the tutors were very friendly, helpful, knew exactly what they were talking about and they also made the course interesting.

How do you feel the qualification has or will benefit you and your company?
The CIMA qualification will be of benefit to me as I will gain the necessary technical expertise to succeed in the present economic climate. I feel it will fill me with the confidence and self-belief needed to become a successful accountant and that it is vital in achieving my long-term career goal of becoming a financial director.

Finally, my qualification will enable me to add value and give something back to the company that gave me the opportunity to succeed and reach my potential.

*For the November 2011 exam sitting.

Other skills needed

Again, employers will be looking for evidence of an important mix of skills, such as:

- commercial awareness and an interest in and understanding of the workings of businesses and the global economy

- a professional, positive and ambitious outlook

- numeracy and analytical skills

- technical (IT) skills

- lateral thinking and logic

- problem-solving skills

- organisational, time management and project management skills

- a calmness under pressure: there is always a deadline looming and there may be lots of balls to juggle at one time as well as working and studying

- the ability to liaise with people at all levels and from all departments, including non-finance members of staff, and to explain complex financial information in a clear manner

- strong communication skills

- influencing and negotiating skills

- language skills, which may be required by some employers

- strength as a team player, as well as strong leadership skills

- the ability to work under your own initiative.

Possible career progression

Finance professionals with a broader business and management understanding are sought after, especially in the current climate where competitiveness is crucial. CIMA is an internationally recognised qualification and you would be valued for your global training and multi-departmental involvement and knowledge. The CIMA qualification affords versatility and adaptability, so you might move up the financial hierarchy into a specialised business or financial analysis position or into a more general commercial or managerial role. Equally, you could move into consultancy or become self-employed. Approximately 20% of FTSE 100 CEOs are CIMA-qualified.

The working environment

The environment is likely to be dynamic, professional and pressurised, but with an underlying routine and work cycle. Routine work will be intermingled with more bespoke reports and projects. You may have to cope with many interruptions and meetings, as well as with many departments demanding attention and information simultaneously. You may have to work overtime to meet a deadline, but there should not be too much disruption to your personal and social life. The typical working week is 44 hours.

Larger organisations can provide more varied experience, but smaller concerns may enable you to work more closely with key decision-makers. Management accountancy can also provide opportunities for travel with multinationals, and CIMA is a valued qualification abroad. Women are somewhat underrepresented, with a male to female ratio of around 65:35, but this is gradually changing. Women are making up an increasing proportion of the new intakes and are now also gaining more senior positions. CIMA's Women in Leadership campaign, which highlights the challenges women face and helps them overcome these obstacles, could be a reason for this.

Typical salaries and benefits

Starting salaries are again dependent on sector, location and organisational size, but tend to range from £23,000 to £26,000. Salaries can increase as you progress through the qualification; the average wage at the operational level is just under £29,000 whereas at the top professional competence level it is £37,000. Post-qualification salaries range from around £25,000 to £57,000, with CIMA finding that members are on average earning around £52,000. At senior level, you might expect to earn £57,000 to £118,000, with just over 11% of CIMA members in the higher salary tier and therefore probably earning £100,000 plus. Bonuses and study packages are commonplace.

Your additional benefits would be similar to those of other professionals, including pension, private healthcare, life insurance, gym membership, childcare vouchers, car allowance, optional holiday and subsidised canteen.

Chartered Institute of Public Finance and Accountancy (CIPFA)

The Chartered Institute of Public Finance and Accountancy (CIPFA) is the only professional UK accountancy body that specialises in finance practices for the public sector. It has a membership of about 14,000 and members can work throughout the public services. By definition, CIPFA members are less likely to practise as accountants for the general public as they tend to work for public-sector departments or in firms that specialise in supplying accounting services to central and local authority organisations.

Profile: Westminster Business School

Westminster Business School, located in the heart of London, is one of the largest centres for business and management education in the UK. The school offers a number of specialist business master's courses, both recognised and accredited by number of professional bodies – namely AMBA (the Association of MBAs), CIPD (the Chartered Institute of Personnel and Development), CIM (the Chartered Institute of Marketing), CMI (the Chartered Management Institute) and ACCA – in the areas of:

- business information management
- economics
- finance and accountancy (with up to seven exemptions from ACCA papers)
- HR management
- management
- marketing
- MBA.

The school is also engaged in conducting applied research that is relevant to all areas of business, much of which has gained an international reputation. Finally, we have built a reputation for enterprise and knowledge transfer in the London region and work with public and private organisations across the UK.

We are London's leading professionally focused and research-engaged business school.

The school is cosmopolitan, having a diverse student population that reflects London's demographic variety, and nearly a third of our full-time students come from outside the UK.

Our staff, too, are drawn from many countries, and every year we welcome visiting scholars and researchers from all over the world. Although we are a school with a strongly international outlook, we also draw on a long tradition of providing part-time courses for Londoners. For nearly 80 years the school has served the needs of busy professionals and businesspeople living or working in the capital, giving our full-time students a unique opportunity to network with the active business community.

Our strong links with London business and government enable us to bring practitioners and headline-makers into the classroom on a regular basis. In turn, we help arrange student placements, internships and mentoring that give our students important hands-on experience and involvement with the world of work.

The school has growing research and consultancy strengths in a range of areas, including employment research, financial services and international finance, leadership, and business strategy. We host conferences, workshops, seminars and other events open to the public, and regard the dissemination of new ideas to the outside world as an important part of our function.

For more information, please visit www.westminster.ac.uk/wbs or contact us at course-enquiries@westminster.ac.uk.

If you are less attracted to commercial arenas and keen to feel that your work is of direct social benefit, then a position in the public or not-for-profit sector, and the CIPFA qualification, could be an option for you.

However, the Big Four and other professional practice firms also have public and voluntary sector specialisms, so ultimately there are a number of areas you can work in if you are interested in CIPFA. Public-sector employers often offer great flexibility and work–life balance, but unfortunately the economic downturn has hit the public sector hard, and instead of recruiting trainees they may be investing in qualified staff. However, they should clearly be keeping one eye on succession-planning. Some sectors, such as health, may offer a choice when it comes to which qualification is studied, but CIPFA is the preferred qualification in general in the public sector.

Chartered public finance accountants ensure the efficient collection and use of funds in public and voluntary sector concerns such as health service trusts, local authorities, housing associations, police and public utility, educational, charitable and central government organisations. You can be managing very substantial resources and budgets, but these are often frustratingly limited for purpose, especially in the current climate of cutbacks. Trainees can be rotated around departments to broaden their experience in larger concerns. While competition for initial training places is still fierce, subsequent positions can be easier to obtain.

Your key tasks would involve:

- financial reporting and control: collating financial data, compiling reports to estimate and review costs and budgets for projects and monitoring investments, spending and cashflow

- allocating funds to projects and departments by assessing service effectiveness and improving financial systems

- conducting internal audits and presenting management information to budget-holders and board members.

Why train with CIPFA? If you want to work in the public sector or public services and utilities, or if you are keen to secure a not-for-profit role, then CIPFA is the most appropriate and relevant qualification as it is the only one tailored towards the needs of modern public services. In the current climate, the ability to stretch resources and reduce costs without loss of service is vital. CIPFA is clearly the expert in public finance management as it has up-to-date knowledge and understanding of the challenges and opportunities that are faced within the sector as well as of the key issues, policies and standards. The syllabus is comprehensive, covering a range of topics from technical finance and accounting to stakeholder communications, ethics and governance, and to management and strategy. The CIPFA qualification also affords flexibility in that you can study at a pace to suit yourself and perhaps your employer.

CIPFA is the only chartered organisation in the world to focus on public finance. It suggests that 80% of training vacancies tend to be found in the public sector and the remaining 20% tend to be with companies serving the public sector, including the Big Four. The latest POB survey reports that 62% of CIPFA's members are currently employed in the public sector, with 3% in professional practice, and 8% in industry and commerce, including public services and utility companies.

CIPFA introduced the new syllabus for the professional qualification in January 2012, developed to complement student work experience and to ensure students get the most out of their studies. There are three stages: professional certificate, professional diploma and the strategic stage.

Each stage is designed to match the experience students are gaining on the job, so students can put theory into practice. One advantage is that studies are very specific to the public sector and you might apply your learning immediately. Study can be done by day release and there are also some online options. The public sector tends to be more flexible regarding examinations.

- The professional certificate (CIPFA affiliate membership) includes examination in financial accounting, management accounting, financial reporting, and audit and assurance.

- The professional diploma (CIPFA associate membership) covers public finance and taxation, public sector financial reporting, governance, public policy and ethics, financial management, business strategy and business management.

- The strategic stage (full CIPFA membership) examines strategic leadership and strategic financial management.

What are the CIPFA entry requirements?

Is a degree required?

While open to graduates in any discipline, 2.i honours are generally sought, and the following subjects may be an advantage:

- accounting or finance

- business or management

- economics or mathematics

- government and politics

- public administration.

It can be possible to gain entry with an HND, especially in one of the above subjects. Relevant study may provide exemptions from the certificate level of the CIPFA qualification; this is assessed on a case-by-case basis.

The minimum entry requirement is two A levels (or equivalent) in any subject and three GCSEs (or equivalent) at A–C grade, which must including English and mathematics at either level.

If you are 21 or over, you can gain entry with three years' work experience and support from your employer.

Other skills needed

Students also need to display a range of other skills, such as:

- numeracy

- spoken and written communication skills

- IT literacy

- analytical and problem-solving skills

- self-discipline and organisational skills

- self-motivation, not just for work, but also to combine the demands of study and work

- team-working.

Possible career progression

Obviously, there are a vast number of bodies that aim to balance public service costs funded by donation or taxation, rather than to maximise profit. Your progression often follows a clear hierarchy, but you should be prepared to be mobile and to relocate if this may help.

In local government, you are likely to be appointed to a specific role after qualification, and you could expect to take responsibility for the overall financial provision of that service or department within a few years. You would progress through taking responsibility for resources or departments of increasing size.

In the longer term, you could move out of the public sector into Public Practice, or even into a broader public sector management consultancy role. Alternatively, you could eventually move into a senior executive position within an organisation, for example as chief executive of a local authority, charity or health service trust.

The working environment

Your average working week would be 35 to 40 hours, but late weekdays and even weekend work may be required at times. However, it is common in the public sector to then take time off in lieu. This is arguably a less pressured and demanding environment than other accountancy specialisms, but it can still have its stresses at busy times, such as the end of the financial year. Public-sector bodies are very open to part-time work, job sharing and flexible working. There tends to be a fairly even male-to-female balance.

Opportunities may be largely in cities and towns, and while the work is office-based you may be required to travel at times, but this is rarely overseas. The work involves a lot of meetings and consultations with different agencies, funders and departments. Although improving, the bureaucracy and relatively slow pace and inefficiency can be frustrating for some people.

Typical salaries and benefits

Starting salaries are said to range from £23,000 to £50,000, with higher pay in London and with the big accountancy firms. A few years after qualification, you should be earning £32,000 to £65,000, and at senior level £35,000 to £100,000. As a local authority director of finance you could earn more than £110,000, plus benefits.

Pension and car allowances are common, and, as with ACA, health insurance, gym membership, share options and bonuses may be part of your package in professional practice.

Other specialist bodies

Association of International Accountants (AIA)

Founded in 1928, the Association of International Accountants (www.aiaworldwide. com) is a lesser known but creditable professional accountancy body that has promoted the notion of 'international accounting'. It encourages trust, clarity and shared standards, and it has a global network of over 7,000 members and 8,500 students and graduates in 85 countries. The AIA qualifications are now recognised in over 30 countries around the world. There are nearly 1,700 members in the UK, working predominantly in companies and 5% in practice. Many of its members are in top positions, ranging from senior management to director level, and represent some of the most major and successful firms.

The minimum entry requirements are similar to those for other professional qualifications: two A levels at grades A–E and three GCSEs at grades A–C. These have to be in five separate subjects, including maths and English. It is important to keep in mind that if you want to undertake the AIA Professional Accountancy qualification and the units involved, you need to have completed a qualification at the same level or one directly below; for example, if you want to take a level 6 unit, you must have completed a level 5 or 6 qualification.

There are three levels of qualification:

1. Certificate in Accountancy

2. Diploma in Accountancy

3. Diploma in Professional Accountancy.

You can do them either as stand-alone qualifications, or complete them all to gain the AIA Professional Accountancy qualification.

Certificate in Accountancy units include: applying financial accounting theory to practical situations; business economics; management accounting; principles of law for accountants; theory and application of the principles of audit; application of the underlying principles of personal and business tax; principles of statistical sources and data collection; and business information processing.

Diploma in Accountancy units include: managing internal and external auditing procedures; the application of company law in financial settings; using statistics as a management tool; designing a management information system; business management principles for accountants; financial accounting for international accountants; and the use of cost control and cost management in operational and strategic decision-making.

Diploma in Professional Accountancy units cover: financial reporting of complex business combinations; financial management with an international perspective; professional practice in auditing; and taxation and tax planning.

Additionally, qualification requires three years' work experience.

Since July 1994, the AIA has been a recognised UK qualifying body for statutory auditors, and it oversees its members in the area of money-laundering. High standards in their professional qualifications are ensured by both internal and external or independent adjudicators.

Like CIMA, this qualification has quite a commercial focus; however, there is one big difference. If you are AIA-qualified you would be authorised to undertake audits. With increased globalisation, this qualification may obviously become more popular. However, while four times as many AIA-qualified accountants work abroad as in the UK, they are still in significantly smaller numbers than ACCA-qualified accountants, who have double the number working overseas.

Chartered Institute of Taxation (CIOT)

The Chartered Institute of Taxation (www.tax.org.uk) was established in 1930 and is incorporated by Royal Charter. This professional taxation institute has about 15,800 members and is the world's largest.

Chartered tax advisers largely work in dedicated departments in high-street accountancy firms and internally in businesses. There are some tax specialist firms, but most offer accountancy and bookkeeping services too. Tax specialists may advise on and produce general accounts for small limited companies, other than audit, as well as rental statements. As a trainee, you may choose the CIOT qualification, or even simultaneously study for ACA and CIOT qualifications if you are working in a taxation division.

Institute of Financial Accountants (IFA)

Established in 1916, the Institute of Financial Accountants (www.ifa.org.uk) is the oldest and largest body of non-chartered accountants in the world. Non-chartered accountants include those who are AAT- and CAT-qualified, and part-qualified individuals.

Membership is aimed at those working in commerce with SMEs, or those who work in small and medium-sized accountancy practices (SMPs) that advise SMEs.

The IFA represents over 10,000 members and students in over 80 countries and it offers financial accountant qualifications and CPD.

Association of Corporate Treasurers (ACT)

The Association of Corporate Treasurers (www.treasurers.org) qualifies, supports and represents its members working in corporate finance, treasury and risk. It professes to be the leading professional body for international treasury, defining standards, promoting best practice and supporting CPD. It is the voice of corporate

treasury and represents its members' interests. It has members in 87% of the
FTSE 100 companies. There is a fast-track route if you are already a qualified
accountant. While an exciting field, treasury is rarely viewed as a starting point
for new graduates.

As a treasurer, you would be concerned with financial policy and strategy, and with
banking, funding and investments, restructuring and balancing debt, equity, foreign
exchange, cost and risk, and ensuring sufficient liquidity to meet potential demand.
In some organisations, you might also take responsibility for pensions, insurance,
property and taxation.

Bookkeeping bodies

Every company is legally required to keep financial records or 'books', whether
manually in ledgers or entered electronically on a computer. Bookkeeping
is a growing and international profession, which involves understanding and
monitoring the workings of a business through the keeping of accurate figures.
Auditors like to know that they have figures they can trust.

As a bookkeeper, you might process data, maintain databases and ledgers,
create cashflow forecasts, complete tax returns for both self-assessment and
VAT, draft final accounts for sole traders and limited companies, and handle
payroll runs.

Should you be organised and methodical, or, in other words, a 'perfectionist', who
gains satisfaction from documenting and entering data and seeing a balanced set
of accounts, bookkeeping could suit you. You may be a school leaver, a graduate,
a mature career-changer or perhaps a stay-at-home mother who wants a small
home-based business.

As a bookkeeper you might work for yourself from home, or you might work
internally with companies of all sizes, even in Public Practice firms – whether large
or small.

Accounting software

It would be sensible to see what software skills appear to be most in demand in the kind of firms that most appeal to you.

Many bookkeeping courses teach the use of popular accounting software such as Sage, QuickBooks, Microsoft Office Accounting 2009, or packages from web-based providers such as Intacct and NetSuite.

Proficiency and experience with the most popular packages may add weight to your CV.

Some bookkeeping courses are partnered with accounting software provider Sage, so you have the opportunity to train with the software and get a thorough knowledge of it.

International Association of Book-keepers (IAB)

Founded in 1973, the IAB (www.iab.org.uk) is the professional and examining body for bookkeepers and has members and students in over 60 countries. It used to focus solely on supporting professionalism and qualifications in bookkeeping, but in recent years the IAB has expanded its offerings to provide essential financial and business skills to those who are entrepreneurs wishing to start or develop a small business or those providing bookkeeping to small businesses. It recognised that few new businesses survive the first two years, often due to poor planning and financial awareness, and that this needed to be addressed.

The IAB now offers over 20 qualifications. Like AAT and CAT, IAB qualifications are respected, stand-alone awards, but you can also use them as a stepping stone towards other professional qualifications. The IAB qualifications can provide eligibility for exemptions from elements of the main professional bodies' examinations: ICAEW, ACCA, CIMA, CIPFA, IFA, AAT and CIPP (Chartered Institute of Payroll Professionals).

The IAB has partnered with accounting software provider Sage to offer a Computerised Accounting for Business qualification, at levels 1, 2 and 3. You can be both IAB- and Sage-qualified through the one course.

Profile: The International Association of Book-keepers (IAB)

What is the IAB?

A leading professional and awarding body . . .

The International Association of Book-keepers was founded in 1973 and until approximately 10 years ago it focused purely on being a professional and examining body for bookkeepers. Building on this, today the IAB is the leading UK and international professional body for those providing bookkeeping and related accounting services to small businesses. Through its broad range of Ofqual-accredited qualifications and its CPD activities, the IAB aims to meet an extensive range of financial skills needs for both young people and adults and to provide essential business skills for those starting or developing a small business.

International . . .

Interest in the IAB is ever-increasing and the IAB continues to grow both in the UK and internationally, with members and students now in five figures and spread across over 60 countries.

An approved supervisory body . . .

The IAB is an approved supervisory body under the UK Money Laundering Regulations 2007 – an important role, meaning that those IAB members who are registered with the association as being 'in practice' are supervised and, in addition, are not required to register separately to be supervised by HMRC in compliance with the regulations.

A committed collaborative partner . . .

The IAB has a significant involvement with, and is a willing partner of, national government and standard-setting bodies, including the HMRC Employment Consultation Forum, the Financial Services Authority (FSA), the Office of the Qualifications and Examinations Regulator (Ofqual), the Financial Skills Partnership (FSP) and the Small Firms Enterprise Development Initiative (SFEDI). Over the last year, working with the FSP and other awarding bodies, the IAB has taken the lead role in the development of bookkeeping units for the new Qualifications and Credit Framework (QCF) in England, Wales and Northern Ireland and has worked very closely with the CIPP in the development of QCF payroll units. In addition, working with the FSP and other awarding bodies, the IAB has played a leading role in the creation of apprenticeships in bookkeeping and a revised payroll apprenticeship.

An awarding body of recognised qualifications . . .

The current range of IAB qualifications now numbers more than 20. In addition to the IAB's 'core' qualifications in bookkeeping, accounting and payroll, the range now includes finance for non-financial managers, small business financial management, business enterprise and business law. In 2008, the levels were expanded so that the IAB now offers Foundation-level qualifications at National Qualifications Framework (NQF) level 1 through levels 2 and 3 to level 4. Several of these qualifications have been granted exemptions by the UK chartered accountancy bodies – ICAEW, ACCA, CIMA and CIPFA. The effect of this is to extend the skills of learners and also to provide complete progression routes from level 1 through to level 4 and on to a range of financial careers including registered bookkeeper, chartered accountant and payroll professional.

Simple steps to becoming a qualified professional bookkeeper

Step 1

Become a student member of the IAB by studying for an IAB professional qualification – safe in the knowledge that IAB qualifications, accredited by Ofqual, are further underpinned by the recognition of chartered accountancy bodies such as ACCA, CIMA, ICAEW and CIPFA. To find an IAB-accredited centre (including distance learning) to help you achieve your goal, visit **www.iab.org.uk/qualifications**.

Step 2

Having achieved your IAB (or comparable) qualification, you can immediately apply for employment or use your skills in your own business or organisation. In summary, by achieving an IAB qualification at the following levels, in either or both manual and computerised bookkeeping/accounting, you have demonstrated that you can:

- **level 1:** enter transactions into bookkeeping records or systems

- **level 2:** maintain records and prepare a trial balance

- **level 3:** make complex bookkeeping adjustments and reconciliations and prepare financial statements for sole traders, partnerships and not-for-profit organisations

- **level 4:** prepare financial statements for limited companies.

Step 3

Once qualified at level 2 or above, you should immediately apply to become a full member of the IAB. This will demonstrate to others your ongoing commitment to maintain and enhance your professionalism. It also gives you access to an extensive range of member benefits, including regular technical updates and member seminars to assist you in keeping up to date with, for example, HMRC and other developments.

Step 4 (just for those setting up in business as a bookkeeper)

Importantly, should you wish to open your own bookkeeping practice (to offer bookkeeping or accounting services to clients), as an IAB member you will be eligible to apply for an additional certificate enabling you to be supervised by the IAB. Registration to be supervised is a statutory requirement under the Money Laundering Regulations 2007, failure to do so being a criminal offence. The IAB provides access to an *IAB Members' Handbook* on its website. This is a **valuable resource for members**, particularly those in practice, and contains useful information and guidance as well as template documents that members may choose to adapt for their own use. If you are considering setting up in practice, below is an quick additional guide to what you may need to consider.

Checklist for starting your own bookkeeping business

- Obtain your qualification and become a supervised IAB member to comply with the Money Laundering Regulations.

- Decide where you are going to work (home, office or premises of clients).

- Obtain an appropriate computer and software.

- Promote yourself, for example through networking, mail-shots and advertising.

- Obtain professional indemnity insurance.

- Decide how much you are going to charge.

- Draw up a letter of engagement and anti-money laundering procedures.

- Register under data protection requirements.

- Continue with your CPD and keep up to date.

Institute of Certified Bookkeepers (ICB)

The Institute of Certified Bookkeepers (www.bookkeepers.org.uk) awards qualifications based on academic attainment and experience and it provides ongoing, free technical support to members. It further promotes bookkeeping as a profession, ensuring that standards are upheld. It is the largest bookkeeping institution in the world, with more than 150,000 members in over 50 countries.

The ICB promotes training in bookkeeping, both as a means of increasing competence and confidence, but also to boost career prospects and as a stepping stone to higher-level financial qualifications. However, the AAT does not allow exemptions for the ICB qualification.

Training providers commonly offer courses in both bookkeeping and Sage, but the ICB has partnered with the Home Learning College to provide dual distance learning course training in a number of areas, from ICB level 2 associate to Sage payroll management. You might sit the paper at home, with a follow-up telephone interview from the ICB.

Association of Accounting Technicians (AAT) bookkeeping course

The AAT (www.aat.org.uk) is discussed in detail in Chapter 5. AAT runs the level 2 Award in Bookkeeping, which provides some exemptions from its Foundation-level AAT qualification. However, it is worth mentioning that the Open University course B190, Introduction to Bookkeeping and Accounting, is said to be similar to the AAT qualification, yet it provides eligibility for more exemptions.

3

Choosing the right path

Making the right choice for you

Everyone should have a clear career direction and action plan. While your personal circumstances, motivations and personality will change over the years, it is a good idea to have a plan that keeps you on track. These changes may contribute to you seeking different things from work at different times as you change, develop and grow, therefore it is sensible to know where you want to aim for and why. Your plan can develop and evolve as you do; it is not something that is static.

Whichever professional qualification you choose, you will still have some scope to switch roles, organisations, specialisms and sectors during your career. However, it is important to remember that the different accountancy routes and qualifications can have a different emphasis and therefore prepare you better for certain roles and career paths than for others. This includes practical skills and marketability. It is crucial to understand the differences to make an informed decision.

It helps to view your career as a journey. The *Oxford English Dictionary* defines 'career' as a person's 'course or progress through life (or a distinct portion of life)'. This provides a greater sense of fluidity and it negates the feeling that you should be sitting on the fence while looking for the perfect round hole for your particular round peg. That said, you do need to start with thorough self-assessment to identify your strengths and interests and therefore decide whether ACA, CIMA, ACCA or CIPFA would best meet your requirements and which sector or type of organisation would best fit with your current motivations, values and personal qualities. Try to be objective and honest about yourself, considering weaknesses and development needs as well as strengths.

Choosing your qualification
Questions to ask yourself

To help you decide which accounting path is right for you, you should consider the questions below, and try to marry your answers up with what you know about the different qualifications.

- Would you envisage yourself as an external adviser or business partner, working in *professional practice* and providing services to client companies, or would you rather be in an *internal* team, working together to ensure the commercial success of the business?

- Are you the *analytical* auditor or financial analyst, or the more *lateral-thinking* corporate financier or management accountant? Are you retrospective or forward-thinking?

- Would you prefer to make best use of *public funds*, or would you prefer to maximise profit for a *commercial* firm?

- Are you prepared to work *long hours* and to *travel* extensively for lengthy periods, or do you want a more *balanced* lifestyle?

- Would you prefer to be *quietly problem-solving*, checking and investigating, or do you see yourself as having *lots of meetings* and dealing with people?

- Do you want to be *tackling problems* and trying to turn a company around, or would you value more routine *maintenance*?

- Do you relish a fast-paced *corporate arena* or would you fit more comfortably into a smaller, more friendly and *personal setting*, where you might be a bigger fish in a smaller pond?

- Are you more excited by the idea of *advising individuals* or *big corporations*?

- Do you want to be a *generalist* or a *specialist*?

- Are you considering a certain role to please someone else because that is *what people from your background do*, or because you cannot think of anything else, or are you considering it because it really *suits who you are* and capitalises on what you represent as a human resource?

- Are you chasing the *money* or the *job*?

- Are you happy to be tied to the *same firm* while you train, or do you want to be able to *change jobs* as you please?

Key differences in qualifications

The main differences between the qualifications are discussed in Chapter 2, but here's a brief reminder.

- ICAEW and ACA qualifications are the choice for the majority in the major accountancy practices as they are seen to have greater prestige and more of a technical slant than other qualifications.

- ACCA provides versatility and is a globally recognised qualification. You are not committed to working for the same employer while studying.

- CIMA is more broadly commercially focused and also more strategic and forward-looking, but you will not be qualified to work in external audit.

- CIPFA is designed for working in the public sector and for maximising public funds and investments.

Obviously, the nature of the work will vary greatly not only according to the qualification but also depending on the role or specialism you ultimately choose. You need to think how you would fit in.

- If you enjoy detailed technical analysis and investigation, you may be particularly attracted to ACA and your dream career might be as an audit partner or forensic specialist.

- If you are innovative and strategic, you may be more drawn to CIMA, or to a future position as a financial director or CEO. A 'big picture' person may favour management accountancy to auditing, or may prefer to work in a smaller practice where you may be more of a generalist, advising SMEs.

- If you are very organised and efficiency-conscious, you may favour ACCA for its performance improvement modules and envisage a future career in financial control, systems or operations management.

- Then again, should you particularly enjoy researching and writing reports, you may see yourself as a financial accountant, and should you really enjoy project work, digging into the detail and finding solutions, financial analysis may hold particular appeal.

- Someone more sensitive, altruistic, and socially and politically minded, might see CIPFA as the only option, or may choose to transfer in-house with a not-for-profit concern after qualification.

- A person who is less 'black and white' and stronger verbally may be drawn to the legislative and interpretive aspects of taxation.

Whichever route you take, there is a role, specialism or sector to match who you are and who you may become in the longer term.

While pay, scope for promotion and level of responsibility may be drivers and motivators in the early years of a career, as you gain more seniority your priorities are more likely to be range of work, level of responsibility and cultural climate, with pay being further down the list. That said, a recent CIPD Employee Outlook survey found that 'increased pay and benefits' (54%) had just nudged above

'improved job satisfaction' as the primary motivator for a job change, no doubt
due to the current economic climate and people feeling the pinch.

Longer-term goals

It is not a case of get into accountancy, qualify and live happily ever after. There
is so much that you can do, but this also means that many people feel lost if they
don't have a goal on which to focus: A levels, degree, traineeship, qualification, but
then what?

While you will not want to plan out and fix in stone your whole working life, you
should at least consider all options and the possible changes you may face. What
could be the next step and how are you going to achieve it? Career development
plans need to be continuously re-evaluated and adapted over time.

You need to answer questions such as: what skills and competencies will I need
to gain for the next stage? What courses are on offer that will help to strengthen
and further my career? What experience should I be trying to gain? What projects
would add weight to my CV? Remember you could move sideways as well as
upwards; you may not want additional responsibility or a leadership position. Keep
up to date with what is happening in the field, and network ... it can still be very
much 'who you know, not what you know' beyond that initial graduate assessment
centre stage.

Know your own strengths, weaknesses and market value. Do not expect busy
people to simply notice what you do. Humbly, quietly and casually point out what
you have achieved or done beyond the call of duty and volunteer for different or
more complex tasks, or bespoke projects.

It can help to consider what your ultimate dream would be. Do you envisage
yourself as a partner in professional practice? Would you rather be the CEO of a
blue-chip company? Would you prefer to oversee government or charitable funds,
and head up the finance department of a local authority? Figure 2 on p. 102 shows
some common career paths, but this also demonstrates the possible movement
between sectors. Chapter 9 discusses post-qualification options in greater depth.

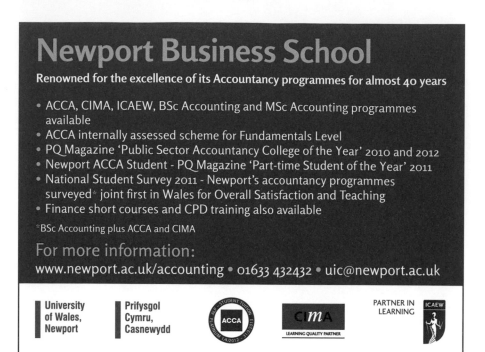

Profile: Newport Business School

University of Wales, Newport

Prifysgol Cymru, Casnewydd

Accountancy tuition from a winning team

Newport Business School (NBS) has been acclaimed for the excellence of its accountancy programmes for almost 40 years; the school has offered tuition for the ACCA and CIMA professional accountancy qualifications since the early 1970s. We are an ACCA Platinum Approved Learning Partner, a CIMA Learning Quality Partner and an ICAEW Partner in Learning. We are also one of only a few colleges nationwide who are able to offer an internally assessed course for all of the ACCA fundamental-level papers. Further, we are the first public-sector tuition provider in Wales to offer ICAEW tuition.

NBS offers undergraduate accounting degrees, an MSc in Accounting and ACCA, CIMA and ICAEW professional programmes. We also offer a suite of finance short courses plus CPD and technical update training.

We have received a number of accolades in recent years. NBS won the prestigious Public Sector Accountancy College of the Year Award at the 2012 and 2010 *PQ Magazine* Awards and a Newport tutor was also shortlisted for the Lecturer of the Year Award in 2012. At the 2011 awards, a Newport ACCA year 4 student won the *PQ* Student of the Year Award. In the CIMA examinations sat in May 2011, a Newport student achieved sixth place in the world for her overall performance in the CIMA strategic-level examinations. Further, accountancy at NBS achieved excellent scores in the National Student Survey 2011 (the sample included the BSc in Accountancy plus ACCA and CIMA). Overall satisfaction was 96%, and scores were above sector averages (often considerably so) in the majority of categories. NBS's provision came joint first in Wales for overall satisfaction and teaching.

The Professional Programmes subject cluster within NBS includes a team of nine qualified accountants who have significant industry and accounting practice experience, as well as significant experience of teaching professional accountancy qualifications. A number of the team are markers for professional body exams; contribute to study note articles published in the professional journals; contribute to online professional student forums; and/or engage in quality control work for the professional bodies, for example assessing exam papers or validating professional courses. We also have significant links with the local and national professional accountancy bodies, and we regularly attend their events (and host their events at NBS).

Question practice tutorials reinforce technical knowledge and exam technique each and every week on all of our professional programmes. The learning environment at Newport is friendly and supportive, and we are able to offer an exceptional level of pastoral support. Further, the study facilities in our new state-of-the-art City Campus are excellent. In sum, the combination of the practical experience and technical expertise of our lecturing team and our excellence in teaching and learning make Newport's accountancy courses very special. We hope that you will soon join us.

Most common career paths

Of course, there are some well-travelled career paths in accountancy. Figure 2 on p. 102 shows you some common routes. It may help you to have a look at the ultimate goal, and work your way back to see what you would need to do to achieve this.

FIGURE 2: Qualification routes

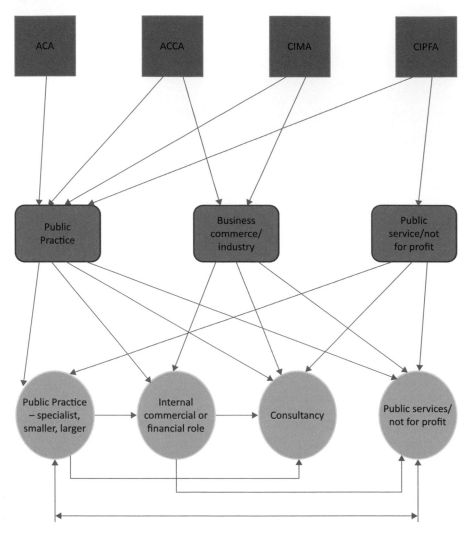

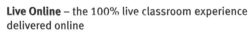

Where you work

Type of firm

The nature of the work will vary greatly according to the firm where you find employment. Not only will the roles and duties differ by firm, but the culture or ethos may be very different too. It's a good idea to consider what type of firm you would like to work in from the very beginning.

Generally, graduate training schemes in Public Practice and blue-chip organisations are better paid, and you would join a cohort of the brightest, most confident and most driven young people. This can be fun, dynamic and exciting, but it is also hard work and pressurised. Some people thrive in this type of environment, whereas others feel that they do not sit comfortably in this aggressive, competitive, materially minded arena. Some firms will not accept examination failure and this can add to the pressure you may already face. If this worries you, it may be worthwhile finding out where you stand before you start.

When working in industry or commerce, there may be less travel and you may be the only trainee in the finance department. This would mean that you have no peers to compare notes with. This could equally be the case in a smaller professional practice, but you may feel more supported and valued than in a large corporation.

Get to know the company

In an article in the *Financial Times* in January 2011, the lead graduate recruitment partner at Deloitte was talking about what both the company and the graduates were looking for in the selection process and choice of firm. He made an interesting point that new and social media have altered the way people research and choose their employers, as more information is becoming available on brand, reputation and ethos. Also, he is being asked about CSR, volunteering and opportunities to 'give something back' by graduates a lot more.

Graduates realise they will have to work hard, but if a firm is a slave-driver it can have negative knock-on effects. It will contribute to employees' stress and underperformance and therefore employees and clients could become disgruntled with the work being carried out, and this could then find itself all over the internet. Graduates select the cultural climate as well as the package and client list; they want to know what it is really like working there, and through the internet and through blogs and social media, they can find out! Obviously, you need to keep an open mind, but asking questions on social media sites can help you gauge other people's views rather than just accepting the promotional company line. Social networking sites such as LinkedIn are also increasingly useful in locating opportunities and building valuable contacts.

Size of firm

The size of the organisation will have an effect on your career direction as well as make a difference to your everyday work life.

A smaller company may be more personal and entrepreneurial and you may be able to gain broader experience and to work more closely with the senior decision-makers. However, it may lack structure and the left hand may never know what the right hand is doing because there may be no established policies, systems or procedures.

When considering working for a small company, it is important to find out what sort of accounting software they typically use. If you are planning to do AAT and then enter a small practice, make sure they have the most popular accounting software, for example QuickBooks or Sage. If they are just using an Excel spreadsheet, you will not be experiencing up-to-date accounting practices. If you have no experience of these popular software packages you may find it hard to progress or move company. That said, this could afford scope for you to make your mark by putting such systems and processes in place.

On the other hand, if you like structure and want to know the right way of doing things, you will perhaps be better off in a large organisation that has clear guidelines, policies and procedures.

Larger organisations may necessitate your taking a more specialised role, and projects may be bigger and more complex. This is in comparison with a smaller firm where you might take a broader perspective and where the role may be more varied and generalist, but where the issues could perhaps be less complex and with fewer stakeholders.

Sector

Different sectors can give you a completely different working experience as they have very different goals and focus. We looked at these in detail in Chapter 1, but now it's important to consider which sector may be right for you. Of course, every organisation is different, but below we have provided some generalisations about different sectors.

Commercial vs public

Commercial firms are interested in the bottom line; they are there to maximise profits and increase market share. On the other hand, public, voluntary and not-for-profit organisations are more concerned with controlling costs and effective management of funds, either from taxation or donations.

The pace in a non-commercial organisation may be slower, and the firm less dynamic. People may be less 'can do' and adaptable, and more regimented in their outlook, working closely to their job descriptions. With emphasis on cost-cutting due to the economic climate, non-commercial sector organisations need to be more efficient and professional. The public sector may suit you better should you seek a more balanced lifestyle, and it may entail more overtly worthwhile and directly socially beneficial work.

Gender

Psychologists have identified 'masculine' and 'feminine' industries and environments. This has nothing to do with sexist stereotypes and whether men or women should be working there. Some women will thrive in an aggressive and objective arena which is said to be 'masculine' – you only have to watch *The Apprentice* to witness this. At the other end of the spectrum, certain males are better suited to working in a nurturing and subjective setting, which is viewed as more 'feminine'.

That said, industries do often correspond to the traditional stereotypes. 'Masculine' industries include engineering, IT, construction, telecommunications and banking, which can be quite no-nonsense and 'say it as it is', whereas 'feminine' areas such as travel, retail and hospitality may favour softer people skills and a more diplomatic approach.

There is also the notion of a 'glass ceiling'. While it is no doubt true that sexist attitudes are still present in many, if not all, sectors, do they prevent women reaching top roles and achieving equal pay? There are valid arguments on both sides of the debate, but it has been suggested that many women choose not to continue up a 'masculine' corporate ladder, but instead leave to work in a smaller, friendlier business. It has further been suggested that if more women could be encouraged to join, progress and remain in 'masculine' companies, the boardroom might benefit from greater empathy, emotional intelligence and a more open climate.

Further decisions

Even in Public Practice, you may have to select not only the division, for example audit, but also an industrial sector in which to specialise even before you start. You will need to be able to put forward a compelling and cohesive argument at interview as to why a certain sector appeals to you and why you think it would suit you.

You will need to look on the firm's website at the sector divisions. For example, PwC breaks audit sectors into:

- insurance and investment management (I&IM)

- banking and capital markets (B&CM)

- technology, information, communication, entertainment and energy (TICE-Energy)

- consumer industrial products and services (CIPS).

In London, instead of the last two, the choice would be between London top tier (LTT – large companies in the FTSE 100) and London mid-tier (LMT – smaller firms).

You need to have several reasons ready as to why you would be interested in and be suited to these specialisms.

Qualifications and exemptions

When deciding what route into accountancy you want to take, you will need to check that you have the academic qualifications to get into your desired training position. To help you determine what is possible, we'll have a look at what you may need in more detail.

Grade requirements

Most graduate trainee accountant roles ask for a 2.i honours degree, but again this is dependent on size, type and sector of the organisation. The selection criteria have tightened over recent years as more people have chosen to go to university, therefore levelling the playing field. Potential employers started to look for a higher degree classification, so everyone started to work harder to achieve that! To differentiate candidates, employers look at UCAS points and usually set a minimum they require. UCAS points were initially introduced as a way of quantifying grades for university entrance, but then employers started to use them too. This is in addition to requiring relevant experience and internships or extraordinary achievements. Relevant degrees are not always essential but are commonly preferred.

Most employers ask for a minimum of 2.i honours and at least 280 UCAS points (around 90% of ACA trainees have a 2.i or a First), although smaller firms and companies will consider a 2.ii. Table 5 below shows how A levels equate to UCAS points: an A* at A level is worth 140 points, an A 120, B 100, C 80 and so on.

However, there may be some flexibility. An example of this is that PwC runs the Inspired Talent programme, which allows graduates with lower entry grades to apply – but you need to be able to demonstrate excellence and 'grit' in an unrelated field, such as being an outstanding sportsperson or having led a fundraising expedition up Everest!

TABLE 5: UCAS tariffs

GCE A level and AVCE	GCE AS Double Award	GCE AS and AS VCE	Points value
A*			140
A	AA		120
	AB		110
B	BB		100
	BC		90
C	CC		80
	CD		70
D	DD	A	60
	DE	B	50
E	EE	C	40
		D	30
		E	20

Source: www.ucas.com/students/ucas_tariff/tarifftables

A higher UCAS tariff is required for more analytical and competitive fields. As an example, PwC requirements are detailed in Table 6 below. The programme aimed at school leavers rather than graduates has a marginally lower tariff requirement.

TABLE 6: PwC requirements

Service line	Qualifications required: UCAS points achieved from top three A levels or equivalent, excluding general/modern studies, and completed in the same academic year	A level grades
Tax	300 UCAS tariff points or equivalent; 2.i degree	BBB
Assurance	300 UCAS tariff points or equivalent; 2.i degree	BBB
Advisory	300 UCAS tariff points or equivalent; 2.i degree	BBB
Financial advisory	300 UCAS tariff points or equivalent; 2.i degree	BBB
Actuarial	320 UCAS tariff points or equivalent (including Maths A level grade B); 2.i degree	ABB
Forensic technology solutions	300 UCAS tariff points or equivalent; 2.i degree	BBB
Strategy consulting	340 UCAS tariff points or equivalent; 2.i degree	AAB
Management consulting	340 UCAS tariff points or equivalent; 2.i degree	AAB

TABLE 6: continued ...

Economic consulting	340 UCAS tariff points or equivalent; 2.i degree (your first degree should be in economics or have a strong economics element; a second degree in economics or a related discipline can prove advantageous)	AAB
PwC legal	320 UCAS tariff points or equivalent; 2.i degree	ABB
Assurance (University Partnership degree programmes)	340 UCAS tariff points or equivalent	AAB
Assurance, Tax, Consulting school and college leavers programme	280, 240, 280 UCAS tariff points or equivalent	BCC

Source: www.pwc.co.uk

Exemptions

Depending on your qualification, you may gain exemptions from the professional qualification you want to study. Many of the professional bodies make exemptions for relevant previous study and some academic institutions have formally partnered with professional bodies and/or accountancy firms. For example, if you meet all the requirement criteria, the Cass Business School's BSc in Accounting and Finance (City University) provides maximum exemptions and credit for prior learning from the ICAEW's ACA qualification. Another example is that completion of either the Open University Certificate in Accounting or the AAT Level 4 Diploma in Accountancy provides exemption from all five of the CIMA certificate levels and you can start studying the professional qualification.

It can even work the other way round. Registration with ACCA automatically provides you with registration for an Oxford Brookes BSc (Hons) in Applied Accounting. On completion of the ACCA fundamental skills papers F1 to F9 and the Professional Ethics module, you may submit an additional research and analysis project to Oxford Brookes University. This is assessed by the University Business School for a degree.

Exemptions are also possible between professional bodies to aid cross-qualification. For instance, you may be ACA-qualified but seek additional CIPFA recognition. By taking two examinations, Public Sector Financial Reporting and Governance plus Public Policy and Ethics, you could complete the professional qualification in six months for CIPFA accreditation. This fast-track option is open to those who are already qualified accountants.

Exemption search

To find out whether your prior courses and study provide eligibility for exemptions, you will need to check the individual professional bodies' websites.

CIMA: www.cimaglobal.com/en-gb/Study-with-us/Exemptions/Exemption-search

ACCA: www.accaglobal.com/en/qualifications/apply-now/exemptions.html

CIPFA: www.cipfa.org/Training-and-Qualifications/Current-students/exemptions

ICAEW: www.icaew.com/en/qualifications-and-programmes/aca/aca-training-in-the-uk/exams/credit-for-prior-learning/apply-for-credits-academic-qualification

Profile: Accounting at London South Bank University

Located just a stone's throw from the City, London South Bank University (LSBU) has held a first-class reputation for delivering high-quality, accredited accountancy courses for over 40 years.

LSBU's Accounting Department is one of the university's largest, offering the perfect launch pad for aspiring accountants at all stages in their career, and the opportunity to study the complete set of 14 ACCA papers required to achieve professional qualification.

While most institutions only train students for external examination, LSBU is proud to be one of only four institutions worldwide to offer a professional internally assessed course to part-qualification, allowing students to achieve their exemptions one by one. This course has been running for over 40 years.

Michael Knight, Head of the Department of Accounting and Finance, says: 'With our new renewed offering of tuition for the final five papers, we can truly deliver one of the most comprehensive accounting portfolios around.

'Each of our courses is designed to propel our students onto the next stage, offering excellent continuity in education. For example, the Foundation degree, which can be topped up to a BA, offers exemptions from the first four ACCA papers, and our flagship BA (Hons) Accounting and Finance degree (which has been running for 20 years) offers exemptions from the first nine. For those who are interested in a career in international accounting, finance, banking or investment, there are master's degrees in these subjects.'

Student satisfaction is high at LSBU, with 90% of full-time first-degree accounting students satisfied with their course (National Student Survey). Courses are taught by award-winning, high-profile academics – for example, this year John Syer, Course Director for First Year Accounting, was honoured as Public Sector Lecturer of Year by *PQ Magazine*, and LSBU's Professor Andrew Chambers recently held a distinguished advisory role in the House of Lords' audit market inquiry.

It's unsurprising that LSBU graduates have gone on to achieve varied and successful careers in public practice, industry and commerce. Recent graduate Elizabeth Adeniran, who achieved a first class BA (Hons) Accounting and Finance degree, is currently on a government-sponsored internship in China and will be taking up a full-time position at Bloomberg in September, and graduate Jemma Hill, who won IFA Top UK Student of the Year in 2010, is now working in working in Deloitte's indirect taxation department.

Michael Knight explains: 'There are many advantages to studying at LSBU: our small class sizes of around 20 students and the delivery of personal tutoring, our central city location generates strong employability links, and we also offer other benefits such as free Mandarin language classes.

'We also have a very active Accounting and Finance Student Society, which hosts numerous employability events and activities.'

To find out more about studying accountancy at LSBU, visit www.lsbu.ac.uk.

All courses are offered full- and part-time:

- Accounting – FdA Foundation degree

- Accounting and Finance – BA (Hons)

- Professional Accountancy Course (PAC) – ACCA

- Accountancy with Finance – MSc.

Courses are accredited by:

- Association of Chartered Certified Accountants

- Institute of Chartered Secretaries and Administrators

- Institute of Internal Auditors.

Case study

Anna Howard, Course Director at London South Bank University

It's a great time to be seriously considering a career as an accountant – the 'stereotypical' grey image the profession once had has become much more colourful.

That's because accountants are performing a wider range of roles in more varied work environments.

Rather than being pure numbers people, they now need to operate as all-round business advisers in areas such as wealth management, business valuation and litigation support – and they interact more closely with clients.

This move away from a pure focus on technical excellence to building stronger client relationships has seen creativity and communication among the additional skills required of the modern-day professional.

Responding to these changes, LSBU has tailored its accountancy courses to meet industry needs, providing high-calibre, well-rounded graduates who have gone on to forge successful careers with the likes of Chevron, the Metropolitan Police, CMG Partners, and the Co-operative Group.

Anna said: 'Studying accountancy here provides a great platform for a successful career, as not only do our students learn accountancy skills, they also gain other employability skills embedded in our courses to make them all-round good employees.

'Being an accountant is not just about numbers. They need to think outside the box and consider the organisational direction and strategy based on the figures they have prepared.

'Communication is also crucial – accountants need to be able to talk to senior management to help with their decision-making, as well as people on the shop floor.'

Here are Anna's top tips for a successful career in accounting.

- Take a practical qualification that's linked to a professional body. You will get the employability skills needed as well as the practical work experience.

- Grab any work experience opportunities while you are studying for a degree. Any job will improve your communication skills and a work ethic looks impressive on a CV.

- Volunteer and get involved with activities outside your course. It demonstrates your character and builds up your CV to tell your story.

- Postgraduate study will demonstrate your willingness to learn and take that extra step – and could make you stand out from the crowd.

- The highest qualification you can achieve will set you apart from other candidates.

Anna worked in accounting before she had a qualification, but realised this would cap her earnings and career progression. She studied a BA in Accountancy and Finance at LSBU – giving her exemptions from many of the ACCA papers – qualified as an ACCA accountant, and then took an MSc at LSBU, before returning to lecture.

She said: 'I really enjoy teaching where I studied and think being a fairly recent student has helped me in the way I communicate with my students.

'Watching them learn and understand something, or helping them solve a problem, is very rewarding. It's hard work gaining a degree in accounting, but definitely worth it.'

She added: 'It's a great profession to enter – accountants are at the heart of how business works, of how value's created and how the world runs.'

Ways of studying

Clearly, you can go quite a long way towards qualifying by selecting a relevant degree and gaining credits towards required practical experience and/or qualifications. However, few people will escape the hard slog of studying while also having a hard day at work. As accountancy is a vast field, there is a lot you have to learn that you may never use, but you still have to learn it.

In professional practice

The ACA qualification will take a minimum of three years in a Training Contract with an authorised employer, who will usually arrange the tuition for you. If you are studying independently, you will need to consider a number of factors when selecting an ICAEW tuition provider:

- programme fees

- structure and combinations of courses and subjects

- how the timing of courses matches your work needs

- pros and cons of residential and non-residential courses

- level of support, assessment and feedback and accessibility of tutors

- other resources, for example online learning

- vicinity of the centre and size of classes.

You must remember that you cannot become a fully qualified ACA chartered accountant as an independent student. You must be in an ICAEW Training Contract with an authorised employer to pass the case-study element of the qualification and to gain the required technical work experience, which are both needed for the ACA professional qualification.

Traditionally, ACA training has involved a mix of weekend and weekday classroom tuition and online self-study. However, some organisations run weekend and online courses, which minimise your time out of the office. This is perhaps more important for smaller firms.

Depending on your academic entry point, Public Practice firms will support ACCA as well as CIMA and CIPFA, in some cases.

In industry

In commerce or industry, there is equal flexibility if you are studying for CIMA, CIPFA or ACCA. Some classroom tuition is likely to be more effective for most people, and you may be supported by peers as well as tutors. Study might be during the evenings or at weekends.

The following list gives examples of tuition providers.

- First Intuition (www.firstintuition.co.uk) runs classroom, online and home study courses for AAT, ACCA, CIMA, ICAEW/ACA and CPD.

- Kaplan Financial (http://financial.kaplan.co.uk) has been a leading provider of financial training for over 50 years and offers classroom, online and distance learning study options. It offers AAT, ACCA, ACA and CIPFA as well as tax and bookkeeping qualifications.

- BPP (www.bpp.com) is a respected provider and offers classroom tuition, virtual learning and distance learning courses leading to ACA, ACCA, CIMA and AAT qualifications.

A list of accredited training providers for each professional body may be found on the tuition provider pages of the professional bodies' websites.

Your experience should be tailored to match the training package provided by the professional body and the accredited training provider. Examples of providers attached to CIMA include companies such as BUPA, Shell, Toyota, Canon and Homebase. It is much easier to follow a training course when you are putting what you are learning into practice at work. Of course, firms do have their own needs and agendas, so sometimes pressing company requirements may take priority over your studies. Equally, you must not allow your focus on passing examinations to prevent you from taking a broader perspective and gaining wider experience in the workplace.

Costs

On formal training programmes, employers will fund your study fees and materials and also provide the required support, study leave and experience you may need. Other employers might part-fund studies, while yet others could expect you to pay for the programme yourself. This can be very expensive, up to £20,000 – which is a lot, especially if you are already loaded down with debt from your first degree.

Professional bodies and training providers may have special offers from time to time, so it is well worth shopping around and doing your research. For example, since 2010 CIMA has waived the first year's subscription for new students.

Accountancy scholarship

Kaplan Financial offers an accountancy scholarship worth over £15,000 to year 11 and 13 students, providing the opportunity for school leavers to study the AAT course and then whichever qualification they choose – ACCA, CIMA, ICAEW or CIPFA – for free. This is irrespective of whether they could secure either a job or funding from the government. Scholarship applications start in September, with the final selection in the spring. See http://financial.kaplan.co.uk for more information on this.

Kaplan also offers some free apprenticeship summer school placements for years 11 to 13. See http://kaplanapprenticeships.co.uk.

Business funding

AAT records show that trainees are nearly twice as likely to pass examinations if they are supported by their employer. A supportive firm might meet the cost of your membership, training provider fees, study materials and books, and may even offer you a bonus or salary increase as a reward for success. Study leave and time to train have also been seen to increase pass rates. That being said, you might alert your employer to this fact and then suggest the following options for how they might recoup some of their costs. Obviously, you will need to create a solid case detailing the benefits to your employer of extending your knowledge of accounting.

Firms might apply for funding to train their staff, for example through Business Link (www.businesslink.gov.uk). There are pockets of funding – for example, one tax practice was able to obtain 40% of the cost of putting its employees through AAT training, as well as obtaining systems and software, from the Rural Development Programme, which is used to distribute funding from the European Agricultural Fund for Rural Development.

Funding for firms for AAT Foundation (NVQ level 2) and Intermediate (NVQ level 3) qualifications is also available through the apprenticeship scheme (www.apprenticeships.org.uk), which is open to all ages of trainee.

For funding in Scotland, Wales and Northern Ireland, see:

- www.skillsdevelopmentscotland.co.uk

- www.new.wales.gov.uk

- www.delni.gov.uk.

Obviously, the advantage of an ACA accountancy Training Contract is that you are earning while studying and fees are paid. For CIMA, CIPFA and ACCA, you may not be so lucky. While still working and earning, you may require some help with training costs; you might be able to get this through a Professional and Career Development Loan (other sorts of loan are available for degree courses).

Professional and Career Development Loan

A Professional and Career Development Loan is a bank loan that you can use to pay for professional training and learning that will enhance your career prospects and job skills. You do not pay interest on the loan while you are studying – the Skills Funding Agency pays it during this time and for one month after you've left your course. Also, you don't have to start paying it back until one month after you have left your course.

Interest rates may vary, but currently such loans typically have a reduced interest rate of 9.9% per annum (typical APR 5%–6%). You can borrow anything between £300 and £10,000 and the loan can help cover up to 80% of the course fees (100% if you've been unemployed for three months), books, travel, childcare, and even living expenses if you are working fewer than 30 hours per week.

You need to be aged 18 or over, with at least three years residency in the UK, and you must intend to stay in the UK or EU post-qualification. The course needs to lead to a stand-alone qualification, not one providing eligibility for the next stage; an example of this would be the Graduate Diploma in Law, which leads to the Legal Practice Course or Bar Vocational Course.

For further information on this, have a look at the Directgov website (www.direct.gov.uk).

Only Barclays and the Co-Op currently offer these loans – so be careful with other banks, which simply let interest accrue while you are studying.

'Time to train' requests

If you work as an employee for an organisation with more than 250 employees, have been employed for at least 26 weeks and are not employed on an official Training Contract, you may be legally entitled to request 'time to train'. For more details check out the Directgov website. Such training has to be pertinent to your professional development and role as well as lead to a qualification. You should follow informal channels for requesting time and training first, and broach the subject sensitively and diplomatically with your boss. Having a solid case for further training and development will help.

While the employer may still pay your salary should they grant your request, they are not obliged to do so. They may propose that you take unpaid study leave or work flexitime in lieu. Your employer will need to consider the national minimum wage and working time regulations when deciding how your training time will be taken.

To count, your 'time to train' request needs to be submitted in writing and dated. It should make clear:

- that it is a request under Section 63D of the Employment Rights Act 1996

- what the training is about

- where and when the study or training would take place

- the training provider and likely tuition and examination fees

- the qualification to which the training will lead

- how this study or training will boost your performance at work and benefit your employer's business

- whether you have made a previous request and, if so, the date of that request, plus details of whether it was emailed or posted.

Should you omit something, your employer may tell you what information is missing and you can resubmit. Although you can make only one request to an employer in a 12-month period, in this case you would not have to wait a year to submit a new request.

Your employer has 28 days to accept and confirm your request in writing or to arrange a meeting to discuss the request further. With the latter, they will have to notify you of their decision within 14 days of the meeting. The dates of the meeting can be extended by mutual consent but must be formally confirmed in writing. You can have a colleague or workplace union representative at the meeting and the employer must allow the meeting to take place in work time and without loss of pay for your colleague. Your 'witness' may confer with you but may not answer on your behalf. Before the meeting you need to prepare a strong case outlining how both your performance and the company's performance will be improved through such training, and how the training will be provided and funded. Your employer will want to discuss how your request might be accommodated practically and flexibly, and any circumstances that might necessitate their support being withdrawn.

Should the employer agree to your request, they should formally notify you in writing. They need to confirm what the training is about, when and where it will take place, who it will be provided or supervised by, the qualification, the implications for salary and working hours, and the funding responsibilities. Should you have mutually agreed to an alternative training option, this will be the one detailed and accepted. If you do not subsequently attend the agreed training, you must formally notify and discuss this with your employer or they could raise a disciplinary action against you.

Your employer can reject your request, or part of your request, for one or more of the following reasons:

- Such training would not improve your performance in that company.

- It would not make their business function more effectively.

Everything you need for ACCA, CIMA and Accounting success!

↘ HD recorded online lectures

Access the full syllabus and extensive study resources 24/7.[†]

↘ Global Campus™

Study at our campuses in London, Birmingham, Manchester, Toronto and Singapore.

↘ Advanced business skills

Add an MBA or MSc to your ACCA/CIMA qualification in just 3 extra modules.

↘ Flexible study

Study full-time or part-time, on campus or online – or blend the two.

ACHIEVE MORE. BECOME MORE.

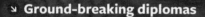

- It would create additional costs.

- It would negatively impact their ability to meet customer demand or improve quality or business performance.

- Your work cannot be delegated to existing staff.

- They are not able to recruit more staff.

- There is no work for you during the proposed working hours.

- The training clashes with intended structural changes.

Should your request be refused, you have 14 days to appeal. You need to set out your case, in writing and dated. Do try talking to your manager and getting them on your side before taking any more drastic formal route. Should you be unsuccessful in your appeal and you feel you have been subject to discrimination, you could ultimately escalate this to a tribunal, but this could put paid to any future progression in that company.

Profile: London School of Business and Finance

LSBF has campuses across the world, a huge range of specialist programmes, students from over 150 countries and an award-winning online platform – all founded on delivering success in accountancy.

From our very first programme offered in 2003, we brought innovation by combining ACCA qualifications with an MBA. This matched business skills with accounting excellence, and we've never looked back.

The number of ways we shape the accountants of tomorrow has grown over the last decade, but our dedication to delivering success hasn't faltered.

Flexible ACCA and CIMA courses

Full-time or part-time, in class or online, our highly experienced tutors are there when you need them. Study at our daytime, evening and weekend classes, or when you like through our online platform. Even blend class and online learning!

Award-winning online platform, powered by InterActive

Access HD recorded lectures covering the entire syllabus, and have live lectures streamed straight to your screen. These are backed by extensive study materials, such as notes, revision packages and mock exams. Dedicated tutors and a global community of students and mentors are also there for you.

Study at a Global Campus™

We have city-centre campuses in London, Manchester, Birmingham, Singapore and Toronto. This gives you the opportunity to match a globally recognised qualification with vital international experience and perspectives.

Combine your ACCA or CIMA qualification with an MBA or MSc

Take your career to a whole new level by adding the advanced business skills of an MBA or MSc in Finance to your ACCA or CIMA qualification. It can take as few as three extra modules, and give you two globally recognised qualifications.

Ground-breaking diplomas that match skills with experience

In partnership with London Metropolitan University, we provide a range of full-time accounting and financial management diplomas. Whether starting from scratch or developing advanced skills, you benefit from unique work-based elements that develop vital practical experience.

The diplomas also prepare you for ACCA or CIMA exam success, while the work-based modules offer an ACCA or CIMA Practical Experience Requirement (PER) head start.

Visit www.lsbf.org.uk/wa or call 020 3005 6188 to discover how we can deliver success for you.

Case study

Maruf Aripdjanov studied at the London School of Business and Finance

Twenty-five-year-old Maruf Aripdjanov is just one of the LSBF success stories. Having studied for his ACCA with LSBF, he is now working as an associate in banking and capital markets at Big Four organisation Deloitte LLP.

Why did you choose to study for your ACCA qualification at LSBF?
Firstly, the LSBF website was very appealing. Having talked to some advisers, I also discovered that the LSBF ACCA courses put great emphasis on future careers.

LSBF better understood what top organisations really look for – and so offered me more than just exam success. Its course developed my interpersonal and communication skills. It also broadened my industry knowledge thanks to way the tutors related topics to real-world business scenarios.

How did LSBF help you achieve success in your ACCA exams?
LSBF put great emphasis on ensuring we learned using relevant business case studies, which really brought the facts and figures to life. It also integrated publications such as the *Financial Times* into our studies, ensuring I could analyse the very latest industry developments. In other words, I could live and breathe finance. This meant I was able to recall and relate information more clearly during my exams.

How has studying your ACCA qualification at LSBF helped your career?
It provided me with in-depth knowledge of accountancy and finance, and meant I was able to formulate and put forward my ideas. LSBF's career department also helped me find relevant work experience, which gave me vital professional confidence.

As I was finishing my ACCA studies, Deloitte LLP offered me a job in its audit division. The skills and experience I gained while at LSBF were pivotal in securing this position. I came to the firm with detailed prior knowledge, helping me take on greater responsibilities from day one.

What is the most rewarding aspect of your current role?
Firstly, it's participating in the auditing of big banks and financial institutions. Secondly, it's the ability to work with some of the best and brightest professionals in their fields.

What advice would you give to new students wanting a career in finance?
My top tip would be to develop strong interpersonal and communication skills together with technical knowledge. Companies look for well-rounded people. This combination will show that you can form and articulate good ideas, as well as build strong professional relationships.

Pass rates for each professional body

While the ICAEW (ACA) examinations are said to be the most stretching, it should be noted that the first-time pass rate is particularly good, and their overall pass rate is also one of the strongest. Of course, this may reflect the fact that the graduate intake is of the highest intellectual calibre, not to mention people who are typically particularly ambitious, competitive and driven. It could further reflect the pressure that many are under, given the Public Practice 'pass or go' policy.

TABLE 7: Accountancy pass rates, 2012

Qualification	First-time passes	All passes
ACCA	57%	55%
CIMA	56%	60%
CIPFA	74%	65%
ICAEW	78%	75%
ICAI	55%	54%
ICAS	n/a	77%
AIA	n/a	9%

Source: POB

Table 7 shows pass rates across the board, while Tables 8 and 9 show ACCA and ACA results for individual papers within the overall professional qualifications. The information is taken from the professional bodies' websites.

ACCA

TABLE 8: ACCA paper results, December 2011

Paper	Pass rate (average = 45%)
F1 Accountant in business	63%
F2 Management accounting	53%
F3 Financial accounting	54%
F4 Corporate and business law	49%
F5 Performance management	38%
F6 Taxation	48%
F7 Financial reporting	56%

TABLE 8: continued ...

F8 Audit and assurance	36%
F9 Financial management	38%
P1 Governance, risks and ethics	51%
P2 Corporate reporting	48%
P3 Business analysis	51%
P4 Advanced financial management	34%
P5 Advanced performance management	29%
P6 Advanced taxation	39%
P7 Advanced audit and assurance	31%

ACCA seems to have fared less well than the other qualifications and concern has been voiced because the average is down from 51% in 2008 to 45% in 2012. The more complex advanced courses, which one might expect to be more difficult, had pass rates of around a third. Of course, these are advanced papers, but it may be that many ACCA students are not on a Training Contract but are studying independently with little employer support or study leave, and possibly little relevant work experience to help consolidate their learning.

Profile: Becker Professional Education – ATC International

By Richard Glover

Preparing accounting professionals for career advancement worldwide with the ACCA qualification

Historically, the credentials and qualifications required for career growth in accounting were, for the most part, determined by geography and which set of accounting principles applied in the jurisdiction of practice. Globalisation is changing that.

As more companies than ever transact business across borders, as the scope of accounting practice continues to broaden, and as International Financial Reporting Standards (IFRS) become more universally accepted, career-focused accountants worldwide are asking themselves some critical questions: Which professional credentials and qualifications are best for my career development, both today and tomorrow?

A global approach to professionalism

Even with the globalisation of commerce and the move towards IFRS, the choice of which professional designation or designations to pursue remains a highly individual one. Although Becker Professional Education has no active role in setting the requirements for the most highly valued accounting credentials and qualifications, we are experts at helping individuals achieve them through our global exam preparation and professional education programmes.

Understanding the ACCA qualification

The ACCA qualification is globally recognised as evidence of a solid foundation of accounting knowledge and is highly valued by accounting and auditing firms of all sizes as well as by organisations across all industries.

	ACCA
Why seek it	• Qualification for professional practice in IFRS-based countries • Global recognition • Versatile qualification for employment in a wide variety of roles in accounting and finance professions • High demand and job stability • Greater earning potential than non-credentialed accountants • Stepping stone to many other career opportunities
Who grants it	The Association of Chartered Certified Accountants (ACCA) is a global organisation of professional accountants with 147,000 members and 424,000 students in 170 countries. ACCA works to strengthen the global profession based on the application of consistent auditing and financial reporting standards; promotes the value of sustainable business; and works to foster the highest professional, ethical, and governance standards.

Who earns it	Individuals who pass a series of demanding exams, meet practical training requirements, and complete a professional ethics module.
How to earn it	• Successful completion of up to 14 exams, depending on exemptions • Exams test knowledge, understanding and application skills of a wide range of disciplines including International Financial Reporting Standards, corporate governance, relevant legislation and taxation, performance and financial management and business strategy. • Completion takes three to four years on average. • First three exams can be taken on demand (computer-based) year-round. All others are currently paper-based taken in June or December. • Can sit at any ACCA exam centre worldwide.

Becker Professional Education has been preparing candidates for success in their ACCA qualifications for over 20 years and has a range of online learning programmes designed to provide you with the support and technical knowledge you need to prepare for the ACCA qualification.

Visit www.beckeratci.com or email info@beckeratci.com for more information.

ACA

TABLE 9: ACA paper results, September 2011 and December 2011

Paper	Pass rate	
	September 2011	December 2011
Business strategy	87.2%	85.5%
Financial reporting	81.1%	73.4%
Financial accounting	86.7%	85.3%
Audit and assurance	85.6%	86.0%
Taxation	93.6%	86.3%
Financial management	85.2%	84.8%
Financial accounting top-up	n/a	93.2%
Average pass rate	86.6%	84.9%

ACA consistently achieves the highest pass rates out of all the accounting qualifications – but do not be fooled: this does not reflect an easier syllabus. Besides being candidates of the highest calibre, ACA trainees are also very well trained and supported.

where people count

Choose First Intuition **for first class service and first time exam success**

♦ Small class sizes

♦ Award winning tutors

♦ Unrivalled tutor support (personal phone and email contact details for each subject tutor)

♦ Flexible study options and choice of study centres

♦ Online recorded lectures free with every classroom course

♦ Free fresh coffee, tea, cakes & fruit every day!

www.fi.co.uk

Find us on Facebook

aat   CIMA   ACCA   PARTNER IN LEARNING

0207 323 9636

info@fi.co.uk

Conway Mews, London, W1T 6AA

Profile: First Intuition

where people count

First Intuition was established in 2007 by a group of experienced tutors and managers with the aim of becoming the first-choice accountancy college for students and their employers. We have quickly established a reputation as one of the most popular colleges in London, with small class sizes and a dedicated tutor team who give students their home and mobile phone numbers and take in extra work for marking, giving students the very best levels of study support. Students come to us from all backgrounds, from those who are simply looking to give their a career a boost, to those on graduate training schemes with the Big Four accountancy firms.

We have study centres in London, Bristol, Cambridge, Maidstone and Reading and, since we were established, have helped thousands of students to pass their professional accountancy exams, achieving pass rates well in excess of the national averages. All our study centres are equipped to an exceptionally high standard, and provide free refreshments to all classroom-based course students.

We run courses for the AAT, ACCA, CIMA and ICAEW qualifications and offer a range of classroom, distance learning and online courses. Our online courses include recorded lectures covering the entire syllabus, breaking down each paper into manageable study sessions. Whichever study method you choose, you receive market-leading study materials and full tutor support.

For more information, please call us on 020 7323 9636 or visit www.firstintuition.co.uk.

Case study

Claire Tomes, First Intuition student

Claire Tomes works as a project manager for UBS and is currently studying for the CIMA Chartered Management Accounting qualification. She has achieved first-time passes in all her exams to date, including a prize for the highest result in the world for paper E1 Enterprise Operations in the November 2010 exam sitting.

'When it came to choosing a tuition provider, value for money, quality of materials and small class sizes were very important.

'I chose to study at First Intuition because it is centrally located and has excellent facilities, with good transport links, internet access and free hot drinks.

'FI has well-structured class notes and tutors set extra homework questions so you can practise what you have learned. Practice exams are part of the tuition and revision courses and are marked by your tutor. Having someone review my scripts and give me one-to-one feedback meant that I could sort out any problems early on so I felt confident when I sat the exam.

'I can strongly recommend First Intuition to anyone studying towards their accountancy exams. All the students I have met at the centre really enjoy their courses. The tutors are really helpful and flexible about being contacted. They provide you with their mobile numbers and email addresses so that they can help you at any point when you are stuck. There aren't many colleges that go that extra mile to help their students.'

What happens if you fail?

In 2009, a ranting email from a PwC trainee, who had been asked to leave because he failed his ACA examinations, went viral. A PwC spokesperson simply commented: 'At the end of the three years, we look at their performance over the three years very carefully and if they have not met the required standard, they would be asked to leave.' The significant factor here is your 'performance over the three years'.

KPMG makes a similar comment on its website: 'KPMG values its people. We give our trainees the best support available prior to the exams and so our exam failure rate is low. However, in the event that trainees do fail they are given the opportunity of a resit, subject to meeting certain criteria.' 'Subject to meeting certain criteria' may perhaps be similar to PwC's 'performance over the three years', but it may also take into account how badly you have failed.

The Training Contract will no doubt state that the firm has the right to terminate employment due to examination failure, and some firms will indeed enforce this. Others may allow you one chance at a resit, but then if you failed again you would be out. You are likely to have to fund the resit yourself and you may not be afforded study leave. Of course, it is best to check all this out during the application stage.

Should you fail and be required to leave, then that could be a good time to see a career consultant to devise a 'plan B'. You may consider a different field of accountancy, or a different firm, sector or professional body. Was accountancy the right choice? Could you have been more motivated in a different specialism? Could you have studied harder? Did personal circumstances interfere and contribute to poor performance? Some firms may even be prepared to fund career counselling as a goodwill gesture when you leave.

CIPFA

The average pass rate for CIPFA is 75%, which is particularly deserving of praise considering that its intake is not as selective – you need only two A levels to study for CIPFA qualifications. The lowest pass rate was 56% for the governance and public policy paper in 2010, but this increased to 80% in December 2011. This reflects the fact that CIPFA regularly reviews its qualification and the performance of its students – and takes action when it is needed. No pass rate fell below 61% in 2011 (see Table 10). However, exam failure is less likely to lead to you losing your job in the public sector.

TABLE 10: CIPFA paper results, June 2011 and December 2011

Stage	Exam	Pass rate	
		June 2011	December 2011
Certificate stage	Financial reporting	75%	55%
	Management accounting	63%	67%
	Financial management systems and techniques	66%	63%
	Financial accounting	61%	73%
Diploma stage	Audit and assurance	71%	76%
	Leadership and management	74%	64%
	Financial and performance reporting	63%	63%
	Governance and public policy	71%	80%
	Accounting for decision-making	73%	75%
	Public finance	76%	75%
	Taxation	86%	84%
	Finance and management case study	75%	68%
	Strategic business management	78%	62%
	Average pass rates	72%	75%
	Submits		43%
	Pending/reworks		10%
	Submit (%)		81%

CIMA

CIMA students scored slightly higher than ACCA trainees, averaging a 58% pass rate, perhaps in similar circumstances. Interestingly, the pass rates were highest for the enterprise operations and financial operations, the fields where accountants would have more day-to-day, hands-on experience. See Table 11.

TABLE 11: CIMA paper results, May 2011

Operational and management levels	UK average pass rates	Global average pass rates
P1 Performance operations	49%	47%
P2 Performance management	52%	46%
E1 Enterprise operations	62%	55%
E2 Enterprise management	53%	49%
F1 Financial operations	59%	57%
F2 Financial management	55%	50%
Strategic level		
P3 Performance strategy	60%	52%
E3 Enterprise strategy	60%	50%
F3 Financial strategy	63%	56%
T4 part B case study examination	63%	59%
Average pass rate	**58%**	**52%**

Profile: Ulster Business School

Do you want to become a professional accountant but don't have an accounting degree?

The Graduate Diploma Accounting programme at the Ulster Business School, University of Ulster, offers you a unique, fast-track, one-year opportunity to become a professional accountant!

Commencing in September each year, this conversion qualification will enable you to pursue a career in accounting from a non-relevant degree subject. You will acquire knowledge of the core areas of accounting and, on successful completion, will have taken the first steps to becoming a professionally qualified accountant.

This programme will be of interest to graduates who wish to gain exemptions from the following professional accounting examinations:

- nine fundamental ACCA examinations

- CA Proficiency 1 (CAP1) examinations of the CAI

- part of the operational- and management-level examinations of CIMA.

You will be expected to have achieved a minimum of a 2.ii Honours degree (or equivalent) in a non-accounting discipline, or an equivalent standard in a professional qualification. In exceptional circumstances, if you do not satisfy these requirements you may be admitted if you can provide evidence of an ability to undertake the programme through the accreditation of prior experiential learning.

To apply, please visit www.ulster.ac.uk/applyonline.

For further information, contact the Department of Accounting, Finance & Economics Office on 028 9036 6906 or at accounting@ulster.ac.uk, or visit our website at www. business.ulster.ac.uk.

Case study

Career change brings employment for accounting graduates

This is the case of a law graduate and a physiotherapist who successfully changed their career paths after completing the University of Ulster's Graduate Accounting Diploma.

Aisling Walls from Hilltown and Ross Hendron from Ballinderry in Northern Ireland have secured Training Contracts with two large accountancy firms.

After graduating with a law degree, Aisling struggled to find work and was unsure of her preferred career path. 'I went travelling for a year to America and when I returned I carried out research online and found the diploma and applied for it,' she said. As a result, Aisling started an internship at Ernst & Young in Dublin with the possibility of being offered a graduate Training Contract if the internship went well.

Meanwhile, fellow diploma student Ross started work in Glasgow on a three-and-a-half-year Training Contract with BDO. 'I was interested in physiotherapy because I'm quite sporty and I like the anatomy side of things, but in practice I found the job wasn't for me at this stage,' explained Ross. 'My friends and family had heard about the course at the University of Ulster and I decided to apply for it. The course is fast-paced, but it was all worth it in the end.'

Course Director Alan Wilson says the Graduate Diploma in Accounting is very popular with both students and employers.

'The diploma is a one-year conversion course for non-accounting graduates to enter a career in accounting. It's an intensive course but the students find it very worthwhile. It gives them a great opportunity to graduate from doing something they have enjoyed and then think about a career in accounting or business,' he said.

'I think our diploma students perform better, in many cases, because they have studied another subject, graduated, and thought about what they wanted to do and then chosen to go into accounting.'

Study tips

Yes, exams are difficult, especially if you have not put in enough effort, but the more you learn and study the easier and less stressful they can become. Some people have to work very hard to achieve the same results as others who always seem to just 'wing it' and do well. Exams depend on individual effort, so you need to identify your abilities and skills. It is important to remember that failure is not accepted, but you need to find the right balance – anything else can be self-defeating. However, almost everyone who trains in accountancy would say that working and studying for a professional qualification at the same time is tough, so you must be totally disciplined. Just remember the rewards you will reap if you are successful.

Set yourself a timetable

It is important to manage your time effectively and prioritise. Which examinations are you due to take and when? What do you need to do to make sure you pass? The answer is to get organised and to have a study plan and a timetable for coursework, revision and practice papers. Create balance – remember to add some breaks, leisure time and rewards for hard work into the picture.

Create a routine

Timetables are very helpful when you're trying to stick to a study routine. When are the days you will be with the tuition providers? Are you a morning or evening person? Would you be better getting up a few hours earlier and studying before work, rather than in the evening after work? Short bursts of study tend to be more productive than long stints, so try not to cram all day on a Sunday. Once you have set your study time, make sure your friends and family know so they don't disturb you, or tempt you away from your work. Limit your distractions – turn off your mobile!

Create a study space

A quiet and comfortable study space can help enormously. You may share a flat with several other professionals or you may have a family, but it is important that you try to create a space that is just yours where you can study undisturbed. Do you really work best with the television on in the background or with music on at full blast? It's probably a good idea to keep the door shut to prevent people wandering in for a chat and interrupting you when you are deep in thought.

How do you learn best?

Do you rely on lists, or do you prefer using mind maps? Depending on the approach you take to studying, there's a style that will work for you.

Find a study partner

Some people prefer to study alone, but others work better with a study partner or in a study group, so you may want to meet up with others from your course or workplace and work on topics together. Talking to and teaching each other can help consolidate learning as well as providing mutual support when it all feels too much.

Don't be too proud to ask for help

It is important that you don't suffer in silence. Some graduates are unaccustomed to struggling, but you may come across obstacles that will cause you problems. If this is the case, you may feel that you are failing or disappointing people or not living up to previous academic successes, but you do not have to feel like this. If you do not immediately grasp something, be prepared to ask questions and to speak to the tutor, or perhaps have a work colleague explain something. You will look more foolish if you fail. That said, accountancy examinations are notoriously hard and very few trainees sail through, and pass everything first time.

Make the most of tutors, study and revision materials

Tuition providers have a reputation to uphold; they want you to pass and they will have created some valuable materials to help you do so. They should also make themselves available to help and may even liaise with your employer should extra time or assistance be necessary. Tuition providers usually offer revision programmes and practice examinations as well; for example, CIPFA has its own exam skills course. Make the most of any study leave you have – don't waste the time and then cram madly at the last minute.

Practice papers

You cannot always predict what will come up, but practice papers will enable you to familiarise yourself with the format of the exams and the type of questions that are used, and to identify any knowledge gaps you might have. Of course, they are good for going over things and revising what you know. If they seem easy, you should gain in confidence. If not, you know that you have more work to do.

Examination day

On examination day, there are many things that you can do to get in the right frame of mind.

- First of all, have a good night's sleep and a hearty breakfast.

- Arrive early with everything you need – it will give you time to gain your composure.

- Try to relax. It is easier said than done, but it does help.

- Read the questions carefully, several times if needed.

- Make sure you manage your time properly. How long do you have for each question? Which questions will take longer? Remember, if you run out of time for a question, try at least to jot down the salient points; if you don't have time to go back to it, you may at least have earned some marks. Another approach is to complete the questions you can do easily and get them out of the way. Which questions earn the most marks?

But remember, if you have studied hard and learned the work, you have nothing to fear! If those other 300,000 qualified accountants could do it, so can you!

4

The Training Contract

What is a Training Contract?

A Training Contract is something that is completely different from an employment contract. It is a signed agreement between the trainee and employer that outlines the terms and conditions of the training to be provided. It also details the criteria that you will also need to meet to remain eligible. Both parties will have a stake in the Training Contract. These contracts are commonly used when the employer is to fund external training by a third-party provider. To study for ACA, you must have a Training Contract. You may also find that firms providing external and internal training for CIMA, AAT or ACCA trainees offer Training Contracts too.

For all ACA or ACCA qualifications with the Big Four and most other Public Practice firms, Training Contracts are mandatory.

Depending on where you start on the qualification, the Training Contract can last anywhere between one and five years, but three years is typical for the average graduate. Training will include hands-on work experience, internal training and external tuition for examinations. But the hard work will pay off – you will be working and earning as well as gaining a professional qualification.

As you would expect, there are typical terms and conditions for a Training Contract, which include the following.

- The firm will provide training, to include all tuition, examination and institute subscription fees.

- The trainee employee must study in their own time, although block study periods can often form part of the training.

- The Training Contract and employment contract will be terminated should the employee fail an exam more than once or fail seriously (usually a mark of 45% or below where the pass mark for the paper is 55%).

Work experience and study components

Accountancy training combines practical work experience with theoretical study, and an accredited training employer will contract to provide you with both. If you can apply to your work what you learn through your studies, it will seem more relevant – and it will help you demonstrate your capability on the job, too. However, for both ACCA and CIMA the practical performance monitoring and experience component do not need to be completed simultaneously.

The different syllabuses and practical requirements

Be clear about what the Training Contract includes, and what it doesn't, before you enter into one. Below, we will examine in detail what your potential employer is actually paying for and its value. We will also cover how the employer should ensure that your practical experience is in sync with the study modules, so you get maximum benefit. You'll see that the different professional bodies have different requirements, which match their slightly different emphasis or slant.

We've also listed the costs of the qualifications. Although these will normally be paid by your employer, you may have to pay for resits, so it's good to have an idea of the costs involved. Your contract should specify what your employer will and will not pay and you should understand this fully in case there are any financial implications.

ACA (ICAEW) professional qualification

Syllabus

The syllabus consists of two parts:

1. the Professional Stage includes knowledge and application modules, combining the core competencies underpinning accountancy with more applied and practical elements

2. the Advanced Stage includes two more complex technical papers and a case study. There is clearly quite a technical emphasis, befitting the initial Public Practice bias. The table below shows the structure in greater detail.

TABLE 13: ACA syllabus structure – Professional Stage

12 papers (six knowledge and six application)			
Application modules		*Knowledge modules*	
Ethics	Audit and assurance (AA)	Ethics	Assurance (AS)
Ethics	Business strategy (BS)	Ethics	Business and finance (BF)
Ethics	Financial reporting (FR)	Ethics	Law
Ethics	Taxation (TX)	Ethics	Principles of taxation
Financial accounting (FA)		Accounting (AC)	
Financial management (FM)		Management information (M1)	

TABLE 12: ACA syllabus structure – Advanced Stage

Two technical integration papers and one case study		
Ethics	Case study (C)	
Ethics	Technical integration	Business change (BC)
Ethics	Technical integration	Business reporting (BR)

Practical component

For the ACA qualification, there is a requirement of 450 days of technical work experience, which you must document in hard copy on the appropriate form (ETWE; Evidence of Technical Work Experience form). This should involve your hands-on commercial or financial experience in one or more of the core technical categories from:

- accounting

- audit and assurance

- financial management

- information technology.

- insolvency

- tax.

It is up to you whether you want to choose one specialism or more – the advantage of choosing just one is that you gain sufficient depth, breadth and progression across that specialism. This can be demonstrated, perhaps through secondments. To help keep you focused and on track you will have six-monthly reviews. If you have prior work experience and qualifications you may be able to claim up to one year's credits and be eligible for a two-year Training Contract. This would therefore reduce the work experience requirement to 300 days. You can see some examples of the common areas of practical activity and technical work experience that can count towards this requirement on the ICAEW website (www. icaew.com).

Examinations

Unless you are an independent student, a training organisation will typically pay exam entry fees as well as tuition fees on your behalf. There are two types of examination.

E-assessments, completed on a computer

By taking the e-assessment you are not restricted to specific exam dates, which gives you and your employer greater flexibility in matching study and assessment timetables with work schedules and business needs. You have two options: you can book the assessment either with an ICAEW-accredited test centre or with a Pearson Vue test centre (www.pearsonvue.co.uk), depending on whether your organisation has established arrangements or not.

- The six knowledge modules of the Professional Stage are available to take by e-assessment.

- Exams are taken at your chosen ICAEW-accredited training centre or Pearson Vue centre.

- Exams last one and a half hours and require a pass mark of 55%.

- If necessary, you may apply to resit the exam immediately, perhaps following discussion with your employer.

- You should receive your results the following day.

Paper-based examinations

- The six application modules of the Professional Stage and the Advanced Stage are tested by paper-based examinations.

- Exams are set and marked by the ICAEW.

- Professional Stage exams last two and a half hours, have a pass mark of 55%, and are taken in March, June, September and December.

- Advanced Stage technical papers last three and a half hours, have a pass mark of 50%, and are taken in July and November.

- Advanced Stage case study exams last four hours, have a pass mark of 50%, and are taken in July and November.

- ICAEW allows four attempts for each Professional Stage module and has removed the limit for the number of tries at Advanced Stage. However, your employer may have different rules so it is important that you are aware of these.

- Results are available five weeks after the exam, and are received either online, by text or telephone, or by post.

Costs and fees

Tuition fees will vary by provider and there can be substantial differences – as much as £300 to £800 on certain modules. Some fees may include learning materials. Fees may not easily be found on websites because they are usually paid by the employer, and, no doubt, are negotiable. Fees for resits may be listed, however, as you, the student, may have to fund yourself if retakes are needed.

A list of tuition providers can be found on the ICAEW site. To give you an example of how much the ACA professional qualification may cost, a London-based tuition provider might charge about £300 for each of the six knowledge modules, £600 for the six application modules and £700 for the three Advanced Stage components. The total amount might be well over £7,000. These prices exclude VAT so the total would be nearer to £9,000, including VAT at 20%. This does not include the ICAEW study materials.

Professional Stage study materials cost £30 per knowledge module, and £45 per application module. Advanced Stage technical integration modules incur a cost of £150 for the double study pack, and the case study is £75, so you need to add another £675. And then you will need to take into account postage and packaging.

On top of this, there will be ICAEW/ACA examination and student fees. Student fees are £165 (plus VAT) per annum. Each knowledge module costs £65 and each application module £85, with exemptions costing the same. The technical integration modules each cost £165 and the case study £255. Additional fees are therefore £1,950 before VAT. The total before VAT is around £9,800 over the three years, assuming there are no failures or resits. These resits cost approximately £260 plus VAT each, but this doesn't include revision courses (which are about £340 plus VAT for each module) or practice examinations. These fees are reviewed annually and therefore subject to change.

ACCA

Syllabus

The syllabus comprises both theoretical and practical assessment, and it covers both Public Practice and business issues.

- Fourteen examinations need to be passed within 10 years (see Table 14 below).

- Thirteen performance objectives need to be monitored and met by an appointed workplace mentor, but this could be before, during or after your studies. Three years of practical work experience is needed before you can become qualified.

TABLE 14: ACCA syllabus structure

Fundamental level		Professional level	
Knowledge module	*Skills module*	*Essential module*	*Options module – two of four papers*
F1 Accountant in business	F4 Corporate and business law	P1 Governance risk and ethics	P4 Advanced financial management
F2 Management accounting	F5 Performance management	P2 Corporate reporting	P5 Advanced performance management
F3 Financial accounting	F6 Taxation	P3 Business analysis	P6 Advanced taxation
	F7 Financial reporting		P7 Advanced audit and assurance
	F8 Audit and assurance		
	F9 Financial management		

Practical component

For the ACCA practical component you will be required to achieve 13 performance objectives in total:

- all nine 'essentials' – performance objectives 1 to 9

- any four 'options' from performance objectives 10 to 20.

ACCA lists these as follows:

Professionalism, ethics and governance

1. Demonstrate the application of professional ethics, values and judgement

2. Contribute to the effective governance of an organisation

3. Raise awareness of non-financial risk

Personal effectiveness

4. Manage self

5. Communicate effectively

6. Use information and communication technology

Business management

7. Manage ongoing activities in your area of responsibility

8. Improve departmental performance

9. Manage an assignment

Financial accounting and reporting

10. Prepare financial statements for external purposes

11. Interpret financial transactions and financial statements

Performance measurement and management accounting

12. Prepare financial information for management

13. Contribute to budget planning and production

14. Monitor and control budgets

Finance and financial management

15. Evaluate potential business/investment opportunities and the required finance options

16. Manage cash using active cash management and treasury systems

Audit and assurance

17. Prepare for and collect evidence for audit

18. Evaluate and report on audit

Taxation

19. Evaluate and compute taxes payable

20. Assist with tax planning.

Examinations

Depending on your educational and vocational experience, you may be exempt from some or all of the initial nine fundamental papers, but most trainees are required to pass a total of 14 exams. These are a mixture of computer-based exams (CBEs), which can be taken at any time to suit you and your employer, and paper-based exams (PBEs), which can be taken in June and December. There are 400 ACCA exam centres around the world.

You may resit as many times as you like, assuming that your employer is agreeable, within the 10-year limit.

Costs and fees

Besides the ACCA membership subscription and examination fees, there are substantial training costs. For example, London-based training providers can charge £400 to £700 for each module, including materials and tuition, plus an additional

£500 to £600 for the revision courses, and a further £245 for the examination rehearsal. So, given that there are 16 modules, qualifying is not cheap and the value of a Training Contract quickly becomes evident. Over the three years, the fees with one such provider could total over £19,000. Fees will no doubt also be subject to annual increases, and perhaps to additional VAT as well. You do need to shop around, though, because these fees can vary substantially, and some tuition providers may include a free practice exam with a revision course.

In addition to this, ACCA charges fees of £77 for initial registration and a £77 annual subscription. Exam fees are subject to change for June and December 2012, and vary depending on when you apply – early, standard or late. If you apply early, the three knowledge examinations cost £55 each, the six skills examinations £69 each, and the seven professional components £81 each. This gives a total of £1,454.

So, assuming you pass first time, the cost of qualifying could be more than £21,000 spread over the three years. However, revision courses and practice exams are clearly optional.

CIMA

Syllabus

Table 15 shows the syllabus and modules for the CIMA chartered management accounting qualification in 2010 (the syllabus changed in January 2010). To achieve chartered status (ACMA, or Associate Chartered Management Accountant), you must pass all levels of the qualification. The initial certificate level includes five modules, and the subsequent professional qualification involves nine modules in total – three modules at each level, including operational, managerial and strategic levels. The final stage, T4, includes IPD, which is work-based practice experience, as well as a case study in the form of an examination. There are no time restrictions.

TABLE 15: CIMA syllabus structure

Certificate in business accounting	CIMA professional qualification (ACMA status)			T4 (formerly TOPCIMA, or Test of Professional Competence in Management Accounting)	
Exemptions from this stage are possible with an accounting degree or AAT qualification	*Operational level*	*Management level*	*Strategic level*	*Part A*	*Part B*
C01 Fundamentals of management accounting	E1 Enterprise operations	E2 Enterprise management	E3 Enterprise strategy	Initial professional development	Case study
C02 Fundamentals of financial accounting	P1 Performance operations	P2 Performance management	P3 Performance strategy	Work-based practical experience	Exam based on previewed and unseen materials
C03 Fundamentals of business mathematics	F1 Financial operations	F2 Financial management	F3 Financial strategy		
C04 Fundamentals of business economics					
C05 Fundamentals of ethics, corporate governance and business law					

Practical component

In addition, you will need at least three years' relevant work-based practical experience before qualifying as a chartered management accountant. Some or all of this experience may be obtained before embarking on CIMA studies, so internships and vacation work while at university can be valuable. On a formal training scheme, the employer should ensure that you receive the correct balance of experience. The CIMA website lists required practical experience, which may be drawn and recorded from any of the three sections listed below, but it must include at least 18 months of core activities.

CIMA lists core practical experience activities as follows.

Area 1: Basic experience

1a.   Preparing and maintaining accounting records

1b.   Statutory and regulatory reporting

1c.   IT desktop skills

1d.   Systems and procedure development

Area 2: Core experience

2a.   Preparation of management accounts

2b.   Planning, budgeting and forecasting

2c.   Management reporting for decision-making

2d.   Product and service costing

2e.   Information management

2f.   Project appraisal

2g.   Project management

2h.   Working capital control

2i.   Risk management and business assurance

Area 3: Supplementary experience

3a.   Financial strategy

3b.   Corporate finance

3c.   Treasury management

3d.   Taxation

3e.   Business evaluation and appraisal

3f.   Business strategy

3g.   External relationships

Examinations

A series of rules govern when and where examinations are taken.

- CIMA Certificate in Business Accounting examinations may be taken at any time at an approved training centre – each centre decides when to offer assessments. The certificate is examined by computer-based assessment.

- All examinations for CIMA professional modules from the operational, management and strategic levels must be taken at CIMA-approved locations at set times of the year (May and November), with resit exams in March and September.

- The T4 (or Test of Professional Competence in Management Accounting) level of the qualification is either a paper-based or computer-based examination and may be taken in March, May, September or November.

- Exams must be taken at only one centre.

Costs and fees

Again, if you are self-funding, you will face substantial cost. There are 11 modules in the professional qualification in total and, with a London-based tuition provider, it may cost as much as £500 to £670 for each module and as much as around £1,500 for T4, plus £500 to £600 for the revision programmes and £245 for the practice examination. Over three years, the cost of these modules could be as much as £18,000, although revision courses and practice exams could be omitted. These amounts are only approximations, and those stated here do not take into account any annual fee increases or additional VAT.

There are also CIMA fees to consider. The first year's subscription is free, but you will still have to pay a registration fee and subsequent subscriptions, which go up to £216 on completion of T4 part B. You will also incur examination fees and, should you be applicable for exemptions, the price will be the same as for the examination modules. Additionally, you would need to pay £70 to register, two years' subscription at £97, five certificate modules at £47 each, six operational and management modules at £79 each, three strategic-level examinations at £85 each, and £101 for the T4. This comes to another £1,329.

Assuming that you are able to pass everything first time, you will still need to find approximately £18,900 over the three years.

CIPFA

Syllabus

The professional qualification takes on average three years to complete and is divided into three parts: professional certificate, professional diploma and strategic. There are 12 modules to be completed in total. They have been designed in consultation with employers to fit together with trainees' work placements and with the hands-on skills they gain from them. A new syllabus and qualification structure were introduced in January 2012 (see Table 16).

- The professional certificate (CIPFA affiliate membership) covers financial accounting, management accounting, financial reporting, and auditing and assurance.

- The professional diploma (CIPFA associate membership) covers public finance and taxation, public sector financial reporting, governance, public policy and ethics, financial management, business strategy and business management.

- The strategic level (full CIPFA membership) examines strategic leadership and strategic financial management.

TABLE 16: CIPFA syllabus structure, January 2012

Professional certificate (affiliate membership)	Professional diploma (associate membership)		Strategic level (full membership)
Financial accounting	Public finance and taxation	Governance, public policy and ethics	Strategic leadership
Audit and assurance	Financial management	Public sector financial reporting	Strategic financial management
Financial reporting	Business management	Business strategy	
Management accounting			

Practical component

CIPFA provides comprehensive guidance notes on the practical component of training, the Initial Professional Development Scheme (IPDS). You can read or download the complete student guide at www.cipfa.org.uk/training-and-qualifications/current-students/IPDS.

You are required to produce a four-part portfolio demonstrating professional development.

1. A log of validated work experience – you must have 400 days in total.

2. Recorded evidence of application and reflection on three of the following:

    - leadership and strategic management
    - strategic and operational financial management
    - financial and performance reporting
    - governance, ethics and values
    - audit and accountability
    - partnerships and stakeholder relations
    - change, risk and project management
    - procurement and contract management.

3. For the final test of professional competence:

    - planning, preparation, delivery and reflection on an oral presentation
    - ability to manage an iterative process
    - management of a long-term planned process.

4. Reflective commentary on your work experience, professional development and goals.

Through an hour-long interview, an assessor will aim to confirm that work documented is accurate, true, and, indeed, your own. You should receive your results within three weeks.

Examinations

There are two sittings of all examinations; they take place in June and November/December at set venues. Certificate and diploma stage exams are all three hours long, except for two half-papers at the diploma stage (on public finance and taxation) that last two hours.

Costs and fees

Again, costs will vary greatly according to the training provider and the method of learning. You can choose from personal tuition, group classes or online learning. London-based training providers often quote about £1,000 per course and there are 13 modules, so the costs can add up. However, with CIPFA itself, you are looking at roughly £600 for each module and £1,500 for the final case study, plus £225 per revision course and £50 for the exam essentials. This totals around £11,370 over the three years. Revision courses and practice exams could be omitted, of course.

CIPFA fees need to be counted, too. Initial registration is £50 and annual student subscriptions are £151 per year (half price if you join after 1 July). If you qualify for exemptions, they are priced at £100 per module. Examination fees for the certificate or diploma stage are £90 per module and the final tests of competence and portfolio submissions are £200 each. So, overall, you are looking at another £50, three yearly subscriptions at £151, 11 modules at £90 and three further payments of £200, which comes to £2,093 – and this is without any retakes or resubmissions.

In all, you are looking at a cost of approximately £13,500 over the three years. Fees will also be subject to increases over the three years and perhaps additional VAT.

Additional in-house training offered

Employers recognise that personal development is vital for their employees so, as well as professional skills and knowledge courses run by external training providers, you are likely to be put through induction programmes and internal courses. An example is the UHY Hacker Young group – it runs courses in accounting, auditing and business-speak in the first two weeks after you join. Similarly, Blick Rothenberg provides early basic grounding in accounting and audit, and, besides this technical training, the group also offers personal and management development courses to build skills such as assertiveness, negotiating and team-working.

Deloitte claims to have a strong learning and development team and reflects this by running intensive internal courses. These courses deal with initial technical training in audit, business skills topics such as personal impact, coaching and client relationships. Some courses are e-learning programmes – over 4,000 e-learning units are delivered via the Skillsoft platform – while others involve simulations, residential facilitator-led training and workshops and classroom-based lessons. Classroom learning is preferred as it ensures that you have the support on hand when you require it.

Besides such induction courses, firms are likely to offer a variety of CPD options to meet your longer-term professional development requirements.

5

Alternative routes into accountancy

On-the-job training

Not everyone wants to or is able to attend university, and the increase in university fees will certainly mean that students are increasingly looking for alternative routes into a career. If you have strong A level grades, which tend to be a minimum of 260 UCAS points, and you have already decided that accountancy is the right career for you, if you are considering a career change, or if you have failed to meet the graduate recruitment criteria, there are on-the-job training schemes available to you. These can speed up the process of professional qualification, so you could be ACCA-qualified within just four years.

PwC runs a school- and college-leavers programme in assurance, tax and business recovery services. In the assurance stream, you would be working on clients' sites on real audit projects and managing your own workload immediately. The work would include checking financial records, collating company information, attending stock counts and testing controls. You would be supported and mentored through the training, studying and working, and you would have the same opportunities as graduate entrants once qualified. There is also the option of further study towards the Oxford Brookes degree (mentioned on p. 110).

The tax programme requires 240 UCAS points and leads to an ATT qualification after two years. You can then take the CTA exams in your fourth year to become a chartered tax adviser.

You can become a certified chartered accountant in four years if you take the business recovery services programme as you will study the ACCA professional qualification. You will be exposed to all sides of the business so no two days will be the same.

KPMG has introduced a school-leaver programme which enables you to train to become a fully qualified chartered accountant while in salaried employment. It is a six-year programme where you will be studying for professional qualifications and an accounting degree from Birmingham, Durham or Exeter University. Grade requirements are ABB grades at A level, plus B grades in GCSE Maths and English Language or equivalent.

Similarly, Deloitte offers the BrightStart school-leavers scheme. There are audit, enterprise risk services, tax, and restructuring services options, and your duties will depend on which branch of the business you choose. You would be working in client-facing roles from day one while studying for examinations and attending internal training events. You would have to meet Deloitte's UK A level entry requirements – these vary from between 240 and 260 points, or 300 to 320, depending on the position you are applying for, and this is not including general studies. The A levels should all be taken in the same year, and at your first sitting. If you have Scottish qualifications, Deloitte accepts five Highers from your fifth year of school, and in some extenuating circumstances, if you don't have five, then four Highers from your fifth year and your best grade from your sixth year will be considered.

Obviously, there are pros and cons for school-leaver entry programmes. On the plus side, you will not incur student debts and you can gain valuable experience while studying. You could always go on to further or higher education at a later stage. However, on the negative side, you may feel that you are committing to a profession very early and you would miss out on the social and personal development aspects of university life. You would also lack the credibility and marketability that have become so important over recent years, although this could change should fewer people go on to tertiary education due to the fee increases.

Accounting technicians

You would not require any formal qualifications to become a trainee accounting technician, but employers will be looking for evidence of:

- good written and oral communication skills

- ability to work in a team, alongside accounting professionals

- ability to multi-task and manage your time

- strong numeracy and literacy

- accuracy

- good attention to detail

- IT literacy.

If you have undertaken relevant study and/or work experience, this will add weight to your CV when applying for traineeships. Gaining a qualification as an accounting technician is an excellent basic foundation and provides credits for professional accountancy qualifications. The main qualifications are as follows.

Association of Accounting Technicians (AAT) qualification

AAT (www.aat.org.uk) is a professional membership body for accounting staff which is sponsored by the following professional chartered accountancy bodies: CIMA, CIPFA, ICAS and ICAEW. It has a global membership of 130,000 in more than 90 countries.

The AAT Accounting Qualification has value in its own right, but is often used as a stepping stone or foundation for chartered accountancy qualifications. All the above professional bodies offer exemptions on the first stages of their professional examinations.

As an accounting technician, you would usually start in a support role working in accounts, bookkeeping, credit control, payroll and audit, or controlling budgets and resources. In time, you might even become self-employed and provide accounts and taxation advice to SMEs. As an accounting technician, you would be able to work in all the same sectors as accountants, which, if you remember, include accounting practice, commerce, industry and the public sector. The Metropolitan Police, Vodafone, the NHS and KPMG are among many firms and organisations that have chosen to put their staff through AAT qualifications. There are no formal entry requirements, although you will need to be numerate and literate.

The qualification is assessed on demonstrated competencies and has three stages:

- level 2 (level 5 Scotland): foundation knowledge and skills covering basic accountancy practices and techniques

- level 3 (level 6 Scotland): intermediate knowledge and skills covering accounts preparation and cash management

- level 4 (level 8 Scotland): higher-level knowledge and skills covering financial management, financial performance and budgeting.

With an accountancy degree, you may go straight to level 4 (level 8 in Scotland) – relevant A levels and HNDs can mean you get exemptions as well. You would have to clarify your starting point with AAT and/or your chosen training provider.

As with all the other qualifications, it does help to be working in finance while studying. It provides you with the necessary year's work experience and evidence of competencies for technician status.

There are 450 AAT Approved training centres in the UK and they all set their own course fees. These are approximately £400 to £800 per level, but can be as much as £1,275. In addition, the AAT admission fee is £38, with student membership being £82 per year. Examinations cost between £35 and £40. Courses are run in a classroom setting, part-time and/or by distance learning.

Profile: Association of Accounting Technicians (AAT)

What does a career in accountancy involve?

Accountancy involves the reporting, recording and analysing of the financial transactions of a business. Accountancy is at the core of every business, whether it is a high-profile international organisation or small and family-run.

What does the AAT Accounting Qualification involve?

AAT offers a fast-track, non-graduate route into chartered accountancy. People who choose this route can avoid up to £9,000 in university debts a year, gain practical work experience as part of their study, and become qualified much faster than those doing a three-year degree.

The AAT Accounting Qualification is a practical, skills-based qualification. Students will learn skills across a range of tasks, from double-entry bookkeeping to management accounts, audit and tax. By the time students have achieved the full AAT Accounting Qualification, they will be equipped with hands-on experience and will have developed work-specific skills.

The qualification is split into three levels, with each level containing theoretical and practical elements. This work-based approach to learning means that AAT graduates are highly regarded in the public, private and not-for-profit sectors.

Case study

Lisa Elsworth, Kent County Council

Lisa Elsworth had a keen interest in accountancy and wanted a credible qualification that would be respected in the finance industry. After finishing her A levels, she elected to start studying through an apprenticeship.

'I went straight from school into my current job at Kent County Council and enrolled to do the AAT Accounting Qualification around the same time. By doing this, I knew I would be working towards a well-recognised qualification at the same time as gaining experience in an accounts role.

'I have been an accountancy trainee for over two and a half years and I have learned about budgeting, finance systems, pensions and general personnel. It's reassuring to know that I am improving my practical skills in these areas every day, something I know I wouldn't have got through a university education. I really enjoy my role – it's so varied and I've learned so much from putting theory into practice and interacting with my colleagues.

'Since finishing my AAT studies, I have progressed onto chartered accountancy and started the ACCA qualification. AAT helped me so much; it gave me the basic level of understanding and great skills so that when I started ACCA I already felt like I had a head start. I plan to qualify without any student debt and by the time I'm 23, quicker than someone who has gone to university.'

With youth unemployment statistics over the million mark and a saturated job market, the AAT qualification offers students the opportunity to combine study and work while gaining experience in a professional office environment.

Visit www.aat.org.uk/accountancy for more information on how to get started or call our student recruitment team on 0845 863 0802.

The ACCA's CAT (Certified Accounting Technician) scheme

The CAT scheme from ACCA (www.accaglobal.com) is now included within the Foundations in Accountancy suite of qualifications. This suite includes the CAT as well as other certificates and diplomas such as the Introductory and Intermediate Certificates in Financial Management Accounting and the Diploma in Accounting and Business.

Since January 2011, CAT students must complete the set practical experience requirements. Again, combining study and practical experience has its benefits. And, as well as the practical experience, while on the CAT scheme you will study towards nine papers, and complete the Foundations in Professionalism.

Open to all ages, the scheme generally takes one to two years, but there is no time limit. No formal qualifications are required, although you will need literacy and numeracy skills. You could get started as a junior accounts clerk from as young as 16 and then possibly secure training as an apprentice. On passing, you would automatically transfer to the ACCA qualification.

Mature students

It is never too late! Just because you did not join in the accountancy profession or one of the big accountancy firms on leaving university does not mean that you cannot have a go further down the line.

Profile: The Training Place of Excellence

Where quality trainings and practical work placements take place

The Training Place
of Excellence
where quality trainings & practical work placements take place

When looking for a job in the accounting field, the first question that most prospective employers will ask you is **'What previous experience do you have?'**

Work experience is key when trying to secure a job. It informs employers of what you have done in the past and how much knowledge you have in your field. Some employers may not even consider your application unless you have the relevant experience.

Here at The Training Place, we believe in providing quality trainings as well as work experience placements to gear people up for the real accounting world. We offer short training courses that are suitable for anyone, whether it is your first step into the accounting world, or you have the theoretical knowledge but not practical experience, or simply to refresh your practical knowledge.

Some of our trainings include:

- **AAT qualifications**

- **Diploma in Accounting, Administration or Business Skills**

- **Excel training**

- **Management Accounts**

- **Sage 50 Accounts**

- **Sage Payroll**

- **VAT.**

Practical work experience is offered with all our trainings.

There is a guaranteed work experience opportunity offered to anyone who attends any of our trainings. This takes place in an accountancy firm where you get the chance to work on live accounts and payroll. The duration of the work placements can be between two months and a year, depending on the number of trainings you attend.

AAT is open to everyone and anyone, and you don't need any previous qualifications to gain this globally recognised qualification. This qualification teaches you necessary accounting skills and knowledge you can apply in the workplace.

AAT QUALIFICATION + WORK EXPERIENCE leads to EMPLOYMENT

Some benefits of studying AAT with The Training Place include:

- **AAT can be an alternative to university**

- **avoid building up student debts**

- **gain relevant accredited qualification**

- **acquire relevant work experience in an accounting firm**

- **gain CV and interviewing techniques**

- **be taught by experienced accountants in practice.**

For further information, call us on 020 7252 9331 or 07958 216021, email us at admin@ thetrainingplace.org, or visit our website www.thetrainingplace.org

Twitter: @Training_Place

Facebook: The Training Place

Remember you have to create your own opportunities to be ahead of the competition!

Case study

Suha studied at The Training Place

Suha, a bio-medical science graduate, joined The Training Place to gain the knowledge and experience needed to work within accounts. The change in career meant that she faced difficulties in finding a role within finance due to her lack of work experience, although she had also completed an accounts qualification – an accounting technician diploma – and has started her ACCA qualification. See below how The Training Place helped Suha in her accounting career.

Where did you hear about The Training Place?
A friend of mine recommended the organisation. I was informed that all the short training courses came with work experience and that it would be a real boost to my CV.

How did the staff assist with your enquiries?
The staff members are very informative and they take their time in explaining the different courses and which ones would be most suitable for each individual situation. All my questions and concerns were dealt with precisely and professionally.

Which training courses did you take?
I started off with the Sage 50 course. I found the course very useful as it relates to the real world and it's not heavily theory-based. After taking the first training, I decided to book

onto four other courses in order to have a good overview of different roles that I could apply for within accounts and boost my chances of employment. I booked:

- Management Accounts

- MS Excel

- Sage Payroll

- VAT.

This gave me a one-year work placement opportunity which has proven to be fully worthwhile.

What did you enjoy most about the training?

Despite my lack of practical knowledge at the time, the tutors were able to guide us through the programme so that we understood how accounting procedures were completed in the real world. All the trainings are delivered in a practical manner and cross-referenced clearly with how they apply in the real world.

What did you enjoy least about the training?

The trainings are all very intense. However, I feel this is also positive, as the quicker I was able to learn the quicker I was able to move on to a full-time position.

How is the work placement assisting in your long-term career?

The work experience gave me an invaluable exposure to the operations of an accounts department and various accounting duties. It increased my practical knowledge and I was able to gain confidence in dealing with accounts on a day-to-day basis. The programme is well structured to help each person progress with their tasks and be able to develop in knowledge and confidence to guide and mentor other new trainees.

This helped reaffirm my knowledge, build further confidence, gain managerial skills, work to tight deadlines and multi-task in dealing with my workload and assisting new trainees with their duties.

While looking for jobs it helped as I was able to explain processes and bring real-life experiences into my explanations. The experience overall has helped me kick-start my career within an accounting role, and is definitely worth it.

For more testimonials and information about the training courses and work placement, please check out our website, www.thetrainingplace.org, or call us on 020 7252 9331.

PwC's Inspired Talent programme was discussed on p. 10. Perhaps you have excelled in a sporting field, made your first million pounds at the age of 16, or raised enormous amounts of money for charity. Perhaps you were the youngest person to cross the Channel on a raft or to play the harp in the Royal Albert Hall. Such achievements demonstrate commitment, determination, dedication, competitive spirit, and a desire to work hard and to win and meet goals. Employers recognise that not everyone can play rugby for England and still have the time to gain straight A grades in their examinations, so they are starting to look for people with notable talent and grit.

Naturally, you do not have to be a star or an academic to gain mature entry. The fact that CIMA, CIPFA and AAT do not set out stringent formal entry requirements means that accountancy can be a possibility if you are looking for a career change. As we may all need to work into our seventies and beyond, and given limited pension resources together with better health and longevity and the legislation against ageism, it means that there are more opportunities for mature applicants. Being mature will mean that you will benefit from greater experience, and you may have better-developed people and communication skills, more ability to handle responsibility, and greater focus, commitment and prudence.

ACCA has a Mature Student Entry Route (MSER) for those over 21 years who are unable to enter via the professional examination route because they fail to meet the academic requirements. The only stipulation is that you must complete and pass the first two papers within two years.

Sponsorship for accountancy degrees

As discussed in Chapter 3 (p. 110), many university degrees provide eligibility for exemptions from professional accountancy qualifications. On the other side of the coin, successful completion of ACCA qualifications would provide automatic eligibility for an Oxford Brookes degree — all you would have to complete is an additional 'Research and Analysis' project. Additionally, several firms and professional bodies are in partnership with particular universities to create salaried or sponsored programmes tailored towards the professional syllabus and providing valuable work placements.

University partnership programmes

The **ICAEW** has partnered with Cardiff, Manchester and Warwick Universities to form the Undergraduate Partnership Programme (UPP), where a practical work experience element is combined with a theoretical course that will help you work towards the **ACA** qualification. The year-long, salaried work placement counts as part of the ACA Training Contract, so post-degree, the qualification will take you two rather than three years.

Cardiff University

BSc Accounting (UCAS code: N400)
http://business.cf.ac.uk/degree-programmes/undergraduate/bsc-accounting

BSc Accounting and Finance (UCAS code: N490)
http://business.cf.ac.uk/degree programmes/undergraduate/
bsc-accounting-finance

Manchester Business School

BSc Accounting (UCAS code: N400)
www.mbs.ac.uk/programmes/undergraduate/courses/accounting

Warwick Business School

BSc Accounting and Finance (UCAS code: NN34)
www.wbs.ac.uk/students/undergraduate/accounting-finance

PwC

PwC has partnered with two academic institutions to offer four-year sandwich degrees that include study towards the **ACA** qualification and three paid work placements where you will earn up to £20,000. Successful completion of these theoretical and practical courses with a 2.i could even ensure you a job offer from PwC.

PwC and Henley Business School at the University of Reading
Four-year BA Accounting and Business (UCAS code: NN41)
www.henley.reading.ac.uk/pwc

PwC and Newcastle University (Flying Start programme)
Four-year BA Business Accounting and Finance (UCAS code: NN14)
www.ncl.ac.uk/flyingstart

Ernst & Young

Ernst & Young is in partnership with **Lancaster University Business School**,
to support and run an ICAS four-year sandwich degree course in BSc (Hons)
Accounting, Auditing and Finance (NN43). This includes up to 18 months' paid
placement in an Ernst & Young office within the UK. By undertaking the course
you would be on the fast track to becoming a qualified chartered accountant.
For more information, visit www.lums.lancs.ac.uk/departments/accounting/
undergraduate/eydegree.

Degree sponsorship

KPMG has partnered with **Durham**, **Birmingham** and **Exeter Universities** to offer
the School Leavers programme. This is a six-year programme that gives the student
the opportunity for paid work experience within the audit department at KPMG,
to study for an accountancy degree at one of the named universities, and the
chance to become a qualified chartered accountant with ICAEW or ICAS. For more
information, visit www.kpmgcareers.co.uk/A-LevelTrainees/default.aspx?pg=1603.

Teach First

PwC, Deloitte and Procter & Gamble are among a number of companies that
have partnered with the Teach First charity. Teach First is an initiative to encourage
the highest-calibre graduates to defer the start of their career and work as a
salaried teacher for two years in a challenging school before beginning their
accountancy career.

As a teacher on the Teach First Leadership Development Scheme, you might feel that you are contributing in a positive way and giving something back, as you would be acting as a change agent and inspirational role model for educationally disadvantaged pupils. Employers recognise the benefit of such intensive leadership training for graduates in terms of enhanced people skills, communication, influencing, presentation, planning and organisational skills. The charity's hope is that graduates who might never have considered a career in teaching will remain in the field and carve out successful careers. However, if this isn't the case, Teach First hopes that they will remain actively involved in an ambassadorial capacity. See http://graduates.teachfirst.org.uk for more information.

6

Work experience and internships

Why are work experience and internships important?

Competition for work experience and internships, let alone graduate programmes, is fierce. Graduate accountancy recruiters are looking not just for exceptional academic achievement, but also for substantial work experience and commercial awareness. As a reaction to this, many students are taking relevant gap year and vacation internships and doing so not only to gain a better understanding of the work and their feelings about it but also to add weight to their CVs. With nearly 50 applications for each position in chartered accountancy, you need to stand out from the crowd, so think about your employability early on. It is estimated that about one-third of trainees will have worked for their employer previously. If you undertake an internship with a larger company, it usually guarantees you an interview or place at an assessment centre for its graduate programmes. Therefore, you can see that going down this route has its advantages.

Some accountancy and business sandwich degree courses offer placement opportunities and you can get support from the university's careers service when looking for these. You should also consider sourcing some holiday internships in accountancy yourself. Internships can lead to job offers, so if you impress your employer you may gain a permanent position upon graduation. If you are not on a sandwich course or you are on an unrelated degree course, you will need to increase your post-degree marketability and knowledge base by locating your own work experience.

Accountancy internships can vary from a year-long 'thick' sandwich placement or several six-week 'thin' placements during academic courses, to salaried vacation work during the long summer breaks. In some cases they may also be taken before or after a degree. They will usually involve supervised practical training. You can apply for some opportunities all year round, but the majority require early application in December or January for the following summer, so you will need to think ahead.

While work experience with the big-name firms can strengthen your CV, experience with smaller firms can also be valuable, and is perhaps more likely to result in you getting a job offer. Besides the blue-chip companies, contact your local high-street practices and the finance departments of small businesses in your area.

Benefits of internships

- You can explore career opportunities, consider which specialisms hold greatest appeal and learn how a firm works.

- You can network and build positive relationships which could help you in the future.

- You might find a mentor to encourage, advise and inspire you.

- You should earn some cash! You should be entitled to the national minimum wage unless you are volunteering with a charity, working for under a year as an obligatory part of an academic course, if you are below school-leaving age or if you're simply 'shadowing' someone.

- You will have the opportunity to gain valuable skills, knowledge and experience, such as people, communication and leadership skills, as well as developing technical competencies and putting theory into practice.

- You will learn about the disciplines of business, and the work experience could even count towards the Practical Experience Requirement (PER) element of your professional training.

How to find internships

You need to make the most of all resources when trying to find an internship — as ever, it can be a case of not what you know but who you know. Personal contacts are still one of the best ways of creating opportunities. Who do you or your relatives know who works in accountancy? Could they put in a good word, pass your CV to their manager, or offer you some work in the holidays themselves?

Apply speculatively. Locate local firms and those of interest through the local chamber of commerce, Business Link, Yellow Pages, or online sources such as www.graduatejobsineurope.com and contact them. Send your CV and a covering letter to them highlighting why you are writing to them, the reason why you want work experience with them, your relevant talents and motivations and the skills you can bring. Always tailor the CV and letter for the organisation to which you are applying, so research them and demonstrate that you have a genuine interest in them and their products or services.

Go online and look on accountancy firms' websites. Many have officially organised internships and many of these are tailored towards different academic levels and stages.

Also, scan the blue chips' websites. A number of companies will offer internships; for example, Procter & Gamble offers finance and accounting internships for students in their penultimate or final year of study.

Internships may be advertised on the jobs pages of the professional bodies' websites (CIMA, ACCA, ICAEW and so on), for example:

- http://trainingvacancies.icaew.com

- www.cipfa.org/Training-and-Qualifications/Become-a-student.

A simple internet search on 'accountancy internships' throws up a number of starting points. There are also websites devoted to internships and recruitment, with many listing vacancies and providing career advice. Helpful sites include:

- http://targetjobs.co.uk

- www.allaboutcareers.com

- www.milkround.com

- www.insidecareers.co.uk

- www.ratemyplacement.co.uk

- www.prospects.ac.uk

- www.internoptions.com (internships in Australia and New Zealand).

Use your university's careers office. They should additionally have relationships with employers and alumni, which you can use to your advantage.

Applying for internships

As you already know, there is tough competition for internship places; therefore, it is important that you put time and effort into each of your applications. You need to demonstrate that you are the candidate for the job, and you do so by targeting the application to that particular company and talking about the relevant skills and abilities you have.

How to write a CV and covering letter

CV

Everyone will tell you to write a CV differently! There is no definitive or right way of writing one, but you must remember that it is your personal self-marketing document and it should be targeted at an audience of accountancy recruiters. Do not think that one CV will do for all companies – a blanket approach will not work. A CV creates the first impression for a recruiter, who is probably inundated with applications and looking for reasons to discard yours, rather than to select it, during the initial sorting. Therefore, your CV should:

- sell yourself and highlight the value you would add to the accounts department or practice

- provide structure and discussion points for an interview

- leave the interviewer with a written record of how you match the person specification. This must include evidence of your skills; it is not good enough just to state that you are a good communicator – you have to back it up.

Having a graduate-level, professional and targeted CV is a must.

Covering letter

Many people focus on their CV and completely miss an opportunity to market themselves further in the covering letter. You have a side of A4 to highlight your strengths and why you think you are the person for the job, so use it!

Covering letters should follow a simple format and should be concise and to the point, flagging why you should be considered.

- **Initial paragraph:** set the scene as to why you are writing and why you have chosen that particular company.

- **Middle paragraphs:** detail your unique selling points and what you have to offer, for example qualifications, work experience, skills and achievements.

- **Final paragraph:** give a conclusion, reiterate your enthusiasm and explain how you intend to follow up your letter.

A lot of time and effort should be put into each application. For more information on how to write a winning CV and covering letter, refer to *You're Hired! How to write a brilliant CV* by Corinne Mills (Trotman, 2009).

If you are not successful in securing an accountancy internship on the first occasion, it can be polite to send a letter thanking the company for its consideration, expressing disappointment but continued enthusiasm and the hope that it will view you more favourably next time!

Making the most of an internship

Beforehand

- Do your homework about the firm so that you do not appear too naive or unprepared. Look on the company's website, as well as at the economic and industry news in trade magazines and newspapers.

- Consider what you want from the placement – contacts, understanding, personal development . . . a job?

- What is the dress code? You could stand outside and watch people coming in and out, but it may be simpler just to telephone and ask! If unsure, it is always better to look professional and smart rather than casual.

During

- Try to make a good first impression: a first impression lasts, and a bad impression can be very difficult to recover from. Arrive early, take notes (if only of names), ask questions, build positive relationships, listen patiently and look interested.

- Do not pretend to understand when you do not. It is better to check, ask for instructions to be repeated and admit that you do not understand what is expected rather than to mess up. Indeed, people may even respect you more if you are prepared to admit that you do not understand.

- Prioritise and show initiative.

- Volunteer for additional tasks and responsibilities in order to raise your profile. Look keen and develop personally and don't act as though making coffee is beneath you.

- Always do your best: ask for regular feedback meetings, which will mean the boss has to monitor and really take notice of what you are doing. It will also help you to correct anything that you may not be doing well.

- Make friends, not enemies. Always be diplomatic as you may be coming back as a trainee accountant in due course.

- Speak up: if you have a good idea or can see that something might be done differently or better, make a suggestion.

- Be professional in both dress and attitude: be on time, do not make personal phone calls, take work seriously, and don't go in with a hangover.

- Have fun: demonstrate that you enjoy the work in accountancy, and that you fit in.

Afterwards

- Request a reference, or enlist your boss as a referee for the future.

- Keep a log of what you did and learned and perhaps what you would or should have done differently. You may be able to detail this for your PER.

- Write a letter of thanks: one accountant was once offered a job because he had been the only intern to have done so! This is an opportunity to praise the boss and the team for their input, leadership, sharing of knowledge and support, but also to remind them of what you were able to contribute. Express your gratitude for having been given the opportunity and state that the experience has made you even more enthusiastic about an accountancy career. Of course, your letter will also provide prompts and an aide-memoire for the experience and achievements you would like them to mention in their reference.

7

Finding your first training role

Whichever route you choose to go down, whether it's a Training Contract, AAT or CAT qualification, or entering the profession straight from school, this chapter will give you the tools you need to get on to your chosen path. At this stage, you will have undertaken internships and involved yourself in a host of extracurricular activities to add weight to your CV, and you will have done your research into the firms, sectors, qualifications and roles in accountancy to decide what type of job you want to apply for. In this chapter, we will give you ideas about where to locate the opportunities you want to apply for, and then give you the tools and advice you need to secure the role.

Locating opportunities

You are probably asking yourself, how do you actually find jobs to apply for? It is very easy to fall into the trap of simply looking for advertised vacancies, but if you are applying for an advertised job, no doubt another 300 people are doing so as well. Suddenly you are competing with all these other candidates and you will have to make sure you stand out from the crowd. It would be easier to get a job through personal contacts, although sometimes this means that you are making less of an active choice about where you want to work or in which specialism or role.

Of course, there are also recruitment agencies. They do some of the work for you, although they may be interested in filling positions instead of your career interests and aims. If this is the case, keep focused. Direct applications are also worth a try, whether it is a speculative approach or a formal application through the company website.

The important thing in this difficult and competitive economic climate is to have a balanced self-marketing campaign where you are exploiting all the approaches we'll give you later in this chapter.

For larger firms you need to go to their websites and search for vacancies and training roles. Some recruit all year round, whereas others have one or two set times per year for accepting applications, for example September and June campaigns.

University careers service

You should make the most of your university careers office. They forge valuable links with local and national employers, and some have databases for networking with alumni who are willing to provide help, advice and information. The university, and indeed the local careers service, has job boards that list vacancies and there will be members of staff you can speak to regarding these opportunities as well as about how they would fit with your career goals and development. Companies are becoming more community focused, which means that they increasingly advertise locally.

Graduate recruitment fairs and events

Graduate fairs are good starting points for contacts and information, and it is always worth taking copies of your CV to leave with exhibitors. You never know, you could even end up with a job!

While networking at recruitment fairs is not an interview, you do want to make a good impression so that the recruiter is keen on hearing from you again. It would be beneficial to dress professionally and smartly – you want them to remember you for all the right reasons. Take a name so that you can write to them afterwards, express enthusiasm and thank the recruiter for their time, help and advice.

Speaking with graduate recruiters can be valuable, both to learn what they are looking for and to practise your self-marketing skills. Remember that you do not have to speak exclusively with accountancy firms – blue-chip companies also have accountancy trainees on their graduate finance stream training schemes. You should take this opportunity to explore the differences between the different sectors and your feelings towards them. Make sure you know your talents, strengths and selling points as well as the competencies the companies value, and put these across succinctly. Prepare as you would for an interview.

Often, there are recent graduate employees in attendance to quiz and to tell you about their experiences and the firm's culture. Obviously this is bound to be positive, but you may gain some insights. Have some questions prepared for those you want to speak to. Arrive early so that you have quality time with recruiters and you stand out, rather than being lost in the masses when the rush starts. The research and information gained may also come in useful during the selection process. If nothing else, you are likely to leave with a bag of freebies!

Lists of such events may be found listed on sites such as www.swat.co.uk, www.milkround.com or www.gradjobs.co.uk. Also, a comprehensive national list of fairs is listed on the Prospects website (www.prospects.ac.uk). Inside Careers has an events calendar for chartered accountancy on their website, www.insidecareers.co.uk.

Milk round

The term 'milk round' was coined in the 1960s and refers to the practice of recruiters 'doing the rounds' and touring the country to present at graduate fairs and entice the students to join their graduate training schemes. University careers services typically organise and host these events and they traditionally occur in the autumn and summer terms.

Milk-round activities have increasingly moved online – this provides wider access for target groups and therefore benefits both students and recruiters. Web-based graduate job boards enable you to compare different schemes, to upload your CV and to apply for specific jobs. See www.milkround.com for more information.

Internet searches

There are so many ways of using the internet in a job search these days, from looking directly at the websites of companies, to looking at newspaper advertisements online, to scanning the professional bodies' websites for jobs, to locating or viewing advertised vacancies with general and traditional recruitment agencies and job sites, and to perusing specialist graduate careers sites with jobs sections.

Traditional recruitment agencies

Vacancies may be found on general recruitment agency sites such as www.reed.co.uk, www.michaelpage.co.uk, www.ambition.co.uk and www.hays.co.uk – simply search in the 'finance and accountancy' sections using keywords such as 'trainee accountant', 'trainee' or 'finance trainee'.

Financial recruitment agencies

There are also specialist financial recruitment agencies, such as www.roberthalf.co.uk, www.rkaccountancy.co.uk, www.cameronwallace.com, www.markssattin.co.uk and www.greenwellgleeson.co.uk. However, some may only deal with qualified or part-qualified accountants. SWAT UK (www.swat.co.uk) recruits for several of the top 50 firms of chartered accountants, which are mostly London-based.

Financial job sites

Some online job sites are dedicated to finance and they may have the facility for you to upload your CV for recruiters to find, or for you to reply to advertised vacancies. These websites include:

- www.gaapweb.com

- www.jobsfinancial.com

- www.accountancyagejobs.com

- www.accountancyjobsonline.co.uk

- www.insidecareers.co.uk.

Graduate job sites

Some job sites specialise in graduate opportunities:

- www.milkround.com

- www.gradjobs.co.uk

- www.prospects.ac.uk.

Media advertisements

Job vacancies can be advertised in newspapers – local or national, hard copy or online. Should none of the listed positions seem quite right, look at which agencies are advertising vacancies and you might identify those to whom you might send your CV for future reference:

- http://jobs.guardian.co.uk

- http://ijobs.independent.co.uk

- http://jobs.thetimes.co.uk.

Social networking sites

This is the internet age, and social media can play a large part in your job search. Use LinkedIn, Twitter and Facebook to look for positions and contacts. LinkedIn has various groups that you might join for networking and many companies now have Facebook pages and Twitter accounts to help you gain insights into the firm and to learn when their next recruitment campaign will start. Companies sometimes even advertise specific vacancies through these media.

However, if you decide to 'like' a company on Facebook or follow it on Twitter, there are a few things to remember. You are networking and researching for a professional career and may be applying for jobs, so it may not be the best idea for companies to be able to access your personal photos and status updates. Always remain professional.

Specialist public sector job sites

For CIPFA opportunities, you might look at specialist public sector job sites such as:

- www.jobsgopublic.com

- www.publicsectorjobs.net

- www.lgjobs.com

- www.jobs.nhs.uk

- www.pfjobs.co.uk.

Professional bodies' job pages

The professional bodies list some vacancies on their jobs pages:

- http://myjobs.cimaglobal.com

- www2.accaglobal.com

- www.icaewjobs.com

- www.cipfa.org/recruitment.

Directories

These can be valuable when you are making speculative applications as they will help identify graduate management training schemes in finance and accountancy.

- TARGETjobs lists employers within their relevant sectors and provides comprehensive details of graduate training schemes: http://targetjobs.co.uk.

- The Milkround website also has an A–Z directory of graduate employers: www.milkround.com/employers.

- *The Times publishes* an annual guide to the 100 top graduate employers: www.top100graduateemployers.com.

Contacts

Never assume that you do not know anyone who could help. Perhaps your neighbour's daughter heads up an accounts department? Perhaps your boyfriend's uncle is a senior partner with loads of contacts in the profession? All you need to do is have a long hard think about it.

There is an etiquette to networking like this; never ask for a job directly, simply ask for information and help, give them your CV in case they should hear of anything, and never leave or hang up until you have several other names of people you might contact next. Do not forget to send a thank-you email, which can sometimes prompt them to remember you or to think of an additional way they might help.

Accountancy trade magazines

These may be valuable for a number of reasons, including their recruitment pages or to simply identify which companies are in the news and potentially recruiting. Of course, reading these will also help with your general knowledge for interviews:

- www.accountancylive.com

- www.accountancyage.com

- www2.accaglobal.com

- www.accountingweb.co.uk.

Apply early

Once you have found positions to apply for, apply in good time. You also need to leave a fair amount of time for completing application forms and application processes as they tend to be lengthy, in-depth and multi-stage. You have put in a lot of time to identify the relevant jobs you want to apply for, so you should be prepared to put a lot of effort into this as well. Early applications may be pushed through more quickly with less of a backlog, potentially speeding up the process.

Training and recruitment mistakes are costly, so, to safeguard you, your potential colleagues and indeed potential clients, the selection procedure is very rigorous. Employers need to know that you have the ability, motivation and personal qualities to do the job and to fit in. The thorough selection process often involves several stages, and more than likely will include:

- an application form

- online psychometric measures (often repeated later to prove that it was really you who took the tests)

- an initial sifting interview (which can be a telephone pre-screening interview)

- a competency-based interview

- a day at an assessment centre.

Application forms

Large firms are increasingly using application forms instead of CVs to sift and sort applicants. CVs can be very varied and it may be hard to compare candidates. Not everyone's CV does them full justice or tells the recruiter what they really want to know. Application forms are specifically designed to give everyone an equal chance, enabling you to sell yourself and to fully demonstrate the desired competencies. They generally cover education, career motivation, positions of responsibility and work experience. They ask you to provide situational, behavioural examples, demonstrating key competencies required for the job. This is where relevant work experience comes in handy, as you can draw upon this to provide the examples.

In most cases these days, the application form is online. The types of forms can vary, so it is important that you understand this before you start. It may not need to be completed all in one sitting, as there will be the facility to save a draft and return to the form later. This is always a good idea, because you might then spot previously unnoticed errors and think up additional or better things to say! Other forms may indeed need to be completed in one sitting, so once you have started you must be prepared to finish it. Of course, you do not want to agonise over this form forever, but you do need to ensure that it does you justice and makes you sufficiently attractive to get you through to the next stage. Be concise because you can elaborate at interview. It pays to have someone else check it over for typos and grammatical errors, so get a friend or a careers adviser to proofread it for you. If you have completed a number of forms, you may cut and paste between them, but you must make sure the copy is not overtly tailored towards a competitor – and don't simply repeat statements that you have read on the company's website or in a brochure!

Real mistakes found on applications for accountancy positions

- 'I was closely involved in every aspect of my former company, right up to its bankruptcy.'

- 'Developed and recommended an annual operating expense fudget.'

- 'Proven ability to track down and correct erors.'

- 'Instrumental in ruining an entire operation for a chain operator.'

Source: University of Kent Careers Advisory Service website

Simple spelling or grammatical mistakes can have very drastic effects because a recruiter could disregard your application if they spot one. Proofreading is a crucial element of completing a form and should never be skipped.

You may already have examples documented on your CV, but you should certainly prepare several for the interview stages to enable you to present hard evidence that you are able to deal with conflict, organise and be self-disciplined, solve problems and work well in a team, as well as other attributes that are relevant to the job you have applied for. What was the situation, what action did you take and how did you behave, and what was the outcome? Remember to answer positively. You can draw examples from personal, leisure, academic and university life – and work experience – depending on what you think best demonstrates your skills. Keep a copy of your application form for future reference, although it can often still be accessed online.

Elements of employability

PwC has a useful 'Employability Guide' which will help you identify and highlight those selling points, qualities and competencies that are valued. These fall under 10 categories.

1. Develop yourself and others through coaching.

2. Communicate with impact and empathy.

3. Be curious: learn, share and innovate.

4. Lead and contribute to team success.

5. Build and sustain relationships.

6. Demonstrate courage and integrity.

7. Manage projects and economics.

8. Be open-minded, able to change and practical.

9. Acquire and apply commercial and technical expertise.

10. Be passionate about client service.

By ensuring that the content of your application fits clearly within one of these categories, you will be creating a well-structured and focused application.

Answers to common questions

Questions should be based on the requirements of the job and therefore reflect what is expected of you should you be successful. Questions that may appear on an application form could include the following.

Please provide us with your understanding of the professional services offered by the firm and, in particular, the work undertaken in your chosen line of service (maximum 150 words).

By asking this, they are looking for you to have an understanding of the role and the company. It is important that you mention drive, commitment, ambition and striving for excellence. Discuss professional training and skills, and dealing with and helping clients. Throw in analytical and problem-solving skills and rising to a challenge. For audit, include words such as 'true and fair' representation, and 'legal requirement'. Emphasise how you might be helping companies to stay buoyant in the marketplace and to appeal more to investors. You would not just be policing but also consulting and advising to remedy weaknesses in processes and so on.

Why are you keen to work for this particular firm?

This can be a difficult question to answer if you have applied for a job in Public Practice because all the Big Four firms offer such great career prospects –

a professional qualification, variety, teamwork, opportunity for progression, learning and responsibility, reputation, scope for travel and secondments, and so on.

You really need to show that you have a valid reason for choosing a particular company, so you should be able to throw in some specific examples of why that firm may be better, or preferable, for you.

- Perhaps it is bigger and more profitable?

- Perhaps it does more for charity or the community?

- Perhaps it has been voted best for disability, training, or women?

- Perhaps it is ranked higher as a graduate employer?

- Perhaps the study timetable is different?

- Perhaps the cultural climate of the firm is more friendly, individualistic or dynamic?

- Does it have a stronger tax or audit department, or has it won awards for corporate finance?

- Maybe it has a higher profile for sustainability?

What research have you undertaken about this firm?

Some of the above answers will obviously demonstrate that you have done your research, but have some facts and figures ready! Do not just have a quick look the night before – study carefully and make notes. Scrutinise the website and brochures, both corporate and careers, and find any recent articles in the press and financial media that you might be able to casually drop into the conversation. Talk to people working in the field and especially for that firm, if you can, and look at professional bodies' websites to ensure that you are fully conversant with the requirements for qualifications and with industry news.

What do you see yourself doing in your first year here?

You must know this! You should be able to demonstrate that you know what you are applying for and why it is right for you. Try telephoning the firms and actually asking what you would be doing in the first and second years – other than studying very hard, of course!

For audit, you might mention substantial travel and being out at clients' sites to reflect that this is OK with you, as well as taking part in audits, learning the ropes and taking increasing responsibility, meeting clients, networking and making new friends and contacts.

We are committed to providing our clients with exceptional services, which add value to their business. From a business perspective, which organisation would be your preferred client and what services do you think we would be providing to enhance the organisation's continued business success (maximum 150 words)?

There are clearly two parts to this question. You need to demonstrate that you understand what makes a good business and what services the firm might offer to improve performance, such as taxation advice, strategy and performance consulting, and internal controls.

When it comes to choosing a client, it may be preferable not to choose a current client; the interviewer may be overly knowledgeable or sensitive. Avoid really technical businesses and perhaps even dotcoms, which may have business models less familiar to more mature recruiters. Select a business you and most others would know, such as a high-street store, but be prepared to talk in depth about it.

Here are some additional questions you might face on the online application form.

- Describe an activity which took you out of your comfort zone.

- Detail an instance when you have had to motivate a team.

- Tell us about when you have applied your learning to make a real difference.

- Describe a situation when you voluntarily took responsibility and showed initiative.

- Outline an instance when you had to put in sustained effort under difficult circumstances.

Psychometric tests

Psychometric tests are scientifically designed and validated measures that aim to objectively assess specific constructs. These could be reasoning potential and typical behaviour. Depending on how much experience you have had with these tests, you could find them daunting or actually quite enjoyable. You may well have already undertaken several cognitive attainment tests (CATs) at school, but you can practise with a number of free tests online. Many people really enjoy the challenges and puzzles involved, especially when individuals are confident in their intellectual capabilities.

Psychometric tests are being increasingly used in the selection processes for large accountancy firms, so it is better that you are prepared for them. There is likely to be an initial, short online screening measure with the online application form, then more in-depth assessments at the assessment centre stage. Some accountancy firms send you the online tests within about two days of you submitting your application. By carrying out these assessments at two stages, the firm is making sure that it was really you who completed the tests in the first place. So don't be tempted to get someone to do them for you – you may as well practise them from the very start.

You should take time to work carefully through the practice tests for these online assessments. Make sure that you are in a quiet space and will not be interrupted when completing the real test. Those candidates who grew up with pencils and notepads could potentially be less comfortable than the internet generation, who may hate to put pen to paper. A way to combat this is to be well organised, with a notepad, calculator, mouse and keyboard arranged conveniently so that no time is wasted reaching past things to work out or mark an answer. The art is for you to go as quickly as you can without making silly mistakes. Try to relax, but don't be surprised if your heart races as you watch the on-screen timer ticking away as you work against the clock. Once you become familiar with the format of the test, it should become easier.

Aptitude measures

Aptitude tests are the most commonly used psychometric assessments within the recruitment process. They use problems presented in different formats, which predict your potential for learning and reasoning through different channels. These might include words (verbal reasoning), numbers (numerical reasoning), or patterns (diagrammatic/perceptual and sometimes logical reasoning). Aptitude measures are standardised to ensure that everyone has the same instructions and therefore the same chance. They are also 'normed' in order to compare your results with the distribution curve of a particular population or group relevant to the assessments (for example, graduates). They are timed and most people are not expected to reach the end. You should work as quickly and accurately as possible and try not to panic.

Most aptitude tests are designed to measure innate potential rather than learned knowledge. As many of the accountancy assessments call for a good grasp of basic mathematics, it would be a good idea to brush up on things such as how to read tables and graphs, calculating percentages and ratios, currency conversions and time/date problems. You may be allowed notepaper and a calculator – this will be made clear to you at the beginning of the assessment. You will have some practice questions before the real thing, and there are a number of sites that enable you to have a go at practice tests ahead of time (see box on p. 196). Make sure that you read each question carefully and that you understand what is required before committing yourself to an answer – multiple choice answers may be similar and are designed to include the most common errors.

It would be advantageous to try to find out ahead of time who publishes the tests, e.g. SHL or Cubiks, so that you know which kind to practise. The latter is said to be particularly difficult, with only around a third of candidates passing. One publication you might find helpful is *You're Hired! Psychometric Tests* (Trotman, 2010).

Firms will generally have a percentile cut-off point, so scores below this will automatically eliminate you. This can place perfectionists at risk, because they often work particularly slowly and carefully through such measures, answering most questions correctly but completing too few to score highly. It is important for you to find the correct balance between speed and accuracy.

Websites for practising psychometric tests

JobTestPrep: www.jobtestprep.co.uk/ernstyoung.aspx

Cubiks: http://practicetests.cubiks.com

Assessment Day: www.assessmentday.co.uk

Criterion Partnership: http://criterionpartnership.co.uk/psychometrics_help

Morrisby Organisation: www.morrisby.com/pages/public/practice-questions.aspx

Knight Chapman Psychological: www.kcpltd.com

Psytech International: www.practicetests.co.uk

Saville Consulting UK: www.savilleconsulting.com/products/aptitude_preparationguides.aspx

SHL Group: www.shldirect.com

Team Focus: www.profilingforsuccess.com/products/profile_yo.php

For a directory of companies offering practice tests: www.psychtesting.org.
uk/directories/companies-that-offer-practice-tests.cfm

Personality measures

Personality tests sample an individual's usual behaviour or style, in order to
predict how you are likely to behave in future situations. Firms rarely use results to
eliminate applicants, but may use them as interview prompts to explore accuracy
and potential concerns. These are self-perception questionnaires that may involve
rating how much a behaviour is like you, or making a forced selection between
several types of behaviour.

There are no right or wrong answers, but it may be worth keeping in mind the
main competencies and requirements of the job. You do not want to fib your way
into a position – ultimately, this will be good for no one if you are not suited to
the work. Selection processes are to protect you as well as the recruiter. While
questions may seem transparent, they are not always assessing what you may think.
The question about whether 'I talk to strangers on the train' could be looking at
unconventionality rather than sociability. The best thing to do is to answer these
questions honestly.

Psychometric tests must be interpreted by trained users. While some are 'normed'
and your results compared with specified populations or groups, others are
'ipsative', which means they simply look at the strengths of various traits within
the individual.

Your first response is usually the most accurate; if you think too long, you will
find it harder to make a decision. The key is to avoid rushing and to take some
time to consider how your chosen behavioural preference looks in the light of
the job requirements.

Sometimes, the choices are scenario-based, which can also give you some insight into what it is like working in the field.

Pre-screen (telephone) interview

Telephone interviews are becoming increasingly common, so it is important to be aware that they may form part of the recruitment process. They take up less time for the interviewer and are a cheaper and easier way of sifting a large number of candidates. You need to put as much effort into a telephone interview and you should prepare and act as though the interview is face to face. On average, they last 10 to 15 minutes.

- Be present and ready to take the call. If you use a mobile, make sure it is charged.

- Remember your posture. Maybe stand rather than be seated – it will ease your breathing and help you to remain alert and focused.

- Smile! Smiling can be sensed by the interviewer and helps you relax.

- Ensure that you have done your research and that you have this and copies of your application form and CV to hand, but don't shuffle the papers around – have them arranged where you can see them easily.

- Make sure that you will not be interrupted by friends, family, dog or phones; shut the door in a quiet room. Make sure you have good reception wherever you choose to take the call if you are using a mobile phone.

- If you cannot hear the question, ask the interviewer to repeat it rather than guess and waffle.

- Speak clearly, concisely and with enthusiasm.

- Don't feel you have to fill awkward silences by blurting something out. Use your listening skills; the interviewer will be making notes on what you have said, so don't feel like you have to keep talking.

Prepare and practise answers to possible questions. Ideally, you would have someone in the field act as interviewer, but a friend or relative could also role-play the interviewer. It is even better if you can find someone who has been through the process with that firm and can provide some inside tips. Your aim is to communicate well and convey motivation.

Example questions

Describe a time you gave a presentation.

Structure your answer clearly and concisely. Set the scene and describe the situation and task you had to undertake. Explain how you went about researching and planning it, what exactly you did and how you put your message across. Highlight that it was well received and describe the positive outcome. Were you offered the job? Did you receive a high mark, or did you win the business or competition? The result should always be included, and if possible link the skills used and what you learned to the job you are interviewing for.

When have you dealt with a difficult situation?

What was the situation? Why was it difficult to communicate? Were you rejecting someone, conveying bad news, dealing with conflict or a sensitive issue? How did you plan and approach it? What did you say, do and feel? What was the result? How was it positive or acceptable? Reflect on what you learned from the experience and how you grew from it.

Why have you applied to us? Why audit (or whichever service line you have chosen)? What do you understand you will be doing in year one?

These have been considered above in the 'application forms' section, but it is important to reiterate that they may also be asked in an interview – so be prepared!

What is your understanding of professional services/of this firm's services?

Obviously, you will need to have researched more than just your service line and you will need to speak coherently about this and about other firms' offerings in general.

Which professional qualification would you chose and why? What is involved in this qualification?

Make sure you know what each qualification entails and have valid reasons for why you are going for CIMA, ACCA, ACA or CIPFA. The earlier chapters should help, but you should also have scrutinised the professional bodies' websites. Have a well-informed decision ready and be prepared to be questioned about it.

It is unlikely you would be able to get feedback from this type of interview, so when you get off the telephone think about your performance and what you could have answered better or differently. Before you come off the telephone, make sure you know what the next step is and that you have a contact name should you need to get back to them in the future.

First interview

After all the hard work up to this point, you should have got through to the first interview stage! The first interview is likely to last between 45 minutes and one hour and is generally face to face. This can sometimes be one to one, or it can be with a panel. The interviewer will usually be a senior manager from your chosen service; a member of staff from HR may also be present. They simply want to know that you want to, and can, do the job and that you will fit in. At this stage, interviewers will therefore be primarily exploring your motivation – why you want to join the firm and what your understanding is about the nature of the work – and getting a feel for you as a person.

The interview is likely to focus on your application form and previous experience, and questions will be standardised (every candidate will be asked the same things to ensure fairness). The key competencies they will be looking for are likely to be as follows:

- ambition and career-mindedness

- commercial awareness and focus

- drive and resilience

- influencing skills and initiative

- leadership and motivation skills

- organisational skills

- problem-solving and analysis

- relationship-building and teamwork.

Additionally, they will be assessing you on:

- image, professionalism, respectability and responsibility

- ethics, integrity, trustworthiness and truthfulness.

Commercial awareness

Commercial awareness is a concept that is bandied around a lot but it is a tricky one to grasp as it can be vast and vague. If you have read business and finance at university, this competency may be taken as 'ticked', but what of humanities, arts, science, engineering and social science graduates?

Everyone has to undertake work experience in year 10 at school, and you may also have undertaken vacation work and paid work during a gap year. Think about the firm you worked for: what did you learn about that company; did it meet the needs of the customer; how did it market itself; what would you have done differently; how could it have developed?

Think about your extracurricular activities. Perhaps you were an active member of a student society or of rag week. How did you market events and attract new members or fundraisers? Did you have to budget, assess costs or act as treasurer?

The easiest way to become aware commercially is to keep up to date with current affairs and business news. You can do this by reading the broadsheets and the *Financial Times*, especially anything pertinent to accountancy and to the firm to which you are applying. If you are short on time, you should register for the *Financial Times'* daily email feed, which summarises the news of the day.

Preparation

- Remind yourself of the desired skills and competencies and list several examples of situations and behaviours that demonstrate these.

- Think about possible questions and practise responses.

- Plan what you are going to wear as well as the route and travel timings. Maybe make a practice run, which will then give you the opportunity to stand outside and see what people are wearing. A checklist of things to take with you will help. Perhaps a clipboard or folder with a copy of your application form and CV, names of interviewers, map and contact details of the firm, company literature, details of referees, diary, notes and pen will help you become focused and organised.

- Prepare some good questions to ask the interviewers.

On the day

The interviewer will remember the beginning and end of the interview session most vividly, so you need to start and finish well. Usually, the opposite occurs because nerves spoil interviewees' performance at first and tiredness contributes to flagging at the end.

- Arrive early so that you can relax and compose yourself.

- Turn off your mobile.

- Think about body language: confident entry, firm handshake, smile, eye contact and face as many interviewers as possible. You can always turn the chair to sit at 45 degrees if necessary, but make sure you are able to see the whole panel – it will help it feel less like facing a firing squad! Remember not to slouch or shuffle; cross your legs at the ankle and relax and breathe normally.

- Take cues from the interviewers' body language as well: nodding shows encouragement, leaning forward shows interest, whereas folded arms and finger drumming can be less positive signs! Work from this and take action.

- The interviewer will make all manner of assumptions about your socio-economic, intellectual, educational and political persuasions in the first few seconds, so look and act the part!

- Listen and do not interrupt.

- Be truthful and positive, but not gushing.

- Do not ramble or gabble. Be specific and stay focused.

- Vary the tone and pace of your voice, and avoid clichés and mannerisms such as 'ums' and 'ers'.

Typical questions, prompts and probes

Practise the following questions and you should be able to handle most questions thrown at you.

- What do you know about our business?

- Why have you decided to apply to us in particular?

- What has been your biggest challenge to date?

- What would you say has been your biggest achievement to date?

- How are you able to juggle your commitments?

- Give me an example of when you have completed a task under pressure and to a deadline.

- Give me two examples of when you worked in a team, one where it was a success and one where you overcame a problem. What was your role?

- Describe a time when you were in a conflict situation. How did you handle it? Explain how you chose to do the correct thing. What was the outcome?

- Tell me about a situation where you have successfully persuaded someone to change their point of view. What was the situation? How did you manage to persuade them? What was the result?

- Your tasks are feeling routine: how do you keep yourself motivated?

- Describe a current issue in the business world.

- Which company do you believe has potential for growth, and why?

- Provide an example of a company that has grown a lot in the last couple of years. What would you advise them to do next?

- In your opinion, what problems are professional services firms currently facing?

- Why are you a good candidate for this position?

- What is your biggest weakness?

- What are your development needs?

- How would your team describe you?

- Describe a complex problem you had to deal with recently. How did you resolve it? How did you ensure that you understood all the facts and had considered all alternative solutions?

- How did you structure your time at university, to ensure that you balanced your study and personal life?

- Why professional services/industry/public sector?

- Where do you see yourself in five years' time? What are your long-term career objectives?

- What is the role of a graduate here?

- Tell us about the biggest mistake you have made. What did you learn from your experience?

- How does this organisation add value to its clients?

- How is assurance divided and in which division would you like to work?

- Tell me what you know about the qualification that you will be studying? What is your preference regarding the professional qualifications? Why have you chosen this particular one?

- Detail a situation when you were working towards a deadline and the parameters were changed. What did you do?

- How would you handle a situation in which you weren't going to meet a deadline?

- Which recent developments have strongly affected the accounting industry?

- What can you tell me about the line of service to which you have applied?

- Discuss a recent piece of financial news that has been in the press.

- Give an example of a time when you had to take corrective action and change your plans. Why was this necessary? What did you do? What was the outcome?

- Describe a time when you had to gather large amounts of data. How did you do this? What systems did you use?

- When have you identified an error due to strong attention to detail? How did you identify the problem? What was the result?

- Give me an example of when you have used your communication skills to meet a client's needs and how you went beyond their expectations.

Questions you might ask

One way to leave a positive impression is to have some really good questions prepared. It is an opportunity for you to get your own questions answered. Remember, an interview is a two-way process – they are finding out about you, but you are there to see if that company fits in with your aims and aspirations. Ask about yourself and the particular role and about the organisation.

- Now you have met me, what reservations do you have? What would be the greatest challenges for me?

- How and when will my performance be appraised?

- This is a structured organisation; what opportunity is there for progression? When is the earliest anyone has been promoted?

- Could you tell me about your time at the company and your career development?

- What scope is there for independence and initiative?

- What percentage of trainees are lost in the first year? First three years? (You don't want to look like you are being critical, but retention rates could be helpful information.)

- What is the policy on examination failures? (This is a tricky question to ask as you do not want to look as if you lack confidence, but you do need to know. Try to find out through other methods first.)

- How would you describe the cultural climate of this firm?

- Where do you see the company going in the next few years? What challenges does it face? Is any restructuring planned?

- Why do you believe I should join this firm rather than a competitor?

- When might I expect to hear and to start? (Ask about this if it hasn't already been discussed.)

- You mentioned xyz earlier – would you tell me more about that, please?

If all your questions have been answered, don't ask them for the sake of it. It would look like you weren't listening if you asked something that had already been covered in the interview.

Assessment centre

This is the last stage in the recruitment and selection process. It often comprises further psychometric tests and interviews, e-tray and group exercises and perhaps a presentation.

Preparation

Take heart in the fact that you have made it to this stage. The first interviewer must have liked you enough to put you forward to the next stage and you must be doing something right. Keep this going.

- All materials for the assessments should be provided, but you may be allowed to use your own calculator if you are more comfortable and familiar with it.

- Check that you have any necessary spectacles, hearing aids and medication.

- Notify the staff of any disabilities or special needs as soon as you can.

Psychometric assessment

The firm may have sent you some practice psychometric tests, but if not you can find them online. See the previous section which has more information on this.

Second interview

The interview tips given on pp.200–7 are equally relevant at this stage – keep in mind the competencies being assessed throughout the day.

Group exercises

- In group exercises, speak clearly and audibly to ensure that you are heard by both other candidates and the assessors.

- Think about the roles in a team and make sure you take one. Are you a leader? Would you be comfortable taking control? You could offer to be scribe so that you take control of and a pivotal role in summarising, decision-making and recording action plans. You could take the role of timekeeper, making sure all aspects of the exercise are covered and in plenty of time.

- Make sure that you repeat the key comments of others to demonstrate that you are listening and then expand them and give your own opinion, suggesting compromises where relevant.

- Don't be overbearing: let others have their say. Ask for votes or group consensus, and make decisions where this cannot be reached.

- Draw other people into the discussion. If there are quieter members of the group, ask them questions or their opinions on what others have said.

- Clearly state what has been proposed and plan the action to be taken, agreeing who will be responsible for what and by when.

- Do not make enemies: fellow candidates may well soon be your colleagues. You are not in competition with them at the assessment centre; you are all being assessed individually and all seeking selection.

In-tray/e-tray exercise

This looks at your approach and ability to manage a sample of tasks similar to those required in the actual job. Usually, you will have a scenario described and will need to appropriately handle emails and requests from various parties and stakeholders as they enter your inbox. This exercise will involve demonstrating your abilities in:

- collation and assimilation of information and statistics

- data analysis

- decision-making

- information research

- organisation

- prioritisation

- sensitive handling of information, and of people who may be demanding or disgruntled.

Information will be given that sets the scene and explains the situation, as well as the roles of various parties. Emails may speed up as the time runs out, putting more pressure on you. This requires good time-management skills.

Tips

- Do not rush! Some questions are devised to mislead and it is easy to jump to conclusions.

- Be diplomatic and upset no one.

- Try a practice e-tray exercise such as the one on the Civil Service website at http://faststream.civilservice.gov.uk/How-do-I-apply/Example-e-Tray-Excercise.

- Read instructions and information carefully to fully familiarise yourself with the situation. Be prepared to shelve emails that you cannot answer due to lack of information, or to make judgement calls where appropriate. Sometimes sitting on the email allows time for the missing bit of the jigsaw to fit into place.

- Double-check any calculations you make.

Written exercise

This will generally involve reading company data and information and making choices and recommendations regarding strategy. You need to be able to defend your choices and arguments. This is where your company and sector research will come in handy.

Tips

- Your writing will need to be audience-specific, and ideally without spelling or grammatical mistakes.

- Manage your time so that you give equal attention to each company or sector.

- Communication skills and logical analysis will be assessed in the way in which you construct the report and argue your points.

Lunch

Remember, you will still be being watched and assessed over lunch. Assessors will want to see how you interact and build relationships with clients, so ensure that you are friendly, charming and polite while you are with other candidates. Again, fellow candidates could soon be your peers!

Presentation

You may be required to give a short presentation. This could be part of a group exercise, in which case you must work together as a cohesive team, or you may be briefed individually ahead of time. Stick to time limits – you want to cover all the important points within the time you have. If you don't get the chance to finish, you don't want to feel like you have missed out. Argue points clearly and concisely and be prepared to defend your claims and recommendations. You are not being assessed on your fancy IT skills, but on your ability to assimilate and understand information and to communicate clearly, logically and persuasively.

Afterwards

You should hear within a few days. If you are unsuccessful, try not to be despondent; congratulate yourself on having made it so far, ask for feedback and aim to learn from the experience.

Case study

Nicola Day, senior associate in assurance at PwC

I started at PwC in April 2009 after completing a summer internship in 2007. The selection process for the internship was exactly the same as for the graduate scheme and so, following the placement, I was offered a full-time role to begin when I finished university.

The first stage of the process was to complete an online application form and an online numerical reasoning test. The application form covered areas such as my academic qualifications and expected university grade, my reasons for applying for the role and other areas such as my outside interests and hobbies. The test was done online and was timed, with a series of short maths-based multiple-choice questions to answer. A good background in GCSE-level maths would have been good enough to pass it.

After getting through the application stage and test, I was invited to my chosen PwC office in Newcastle. Here, I took two further tests and took part in a group discussion. We were presented with some brief information beforehand and given time to prepare specific points to discuss. There were four people in the group and the assessors observed us putting forward our points and listening to others.

After the group assessment, I was interviewed by a manager in my chosen department, assurance. During the interview I was mainly asked why I wanted to work for PwC and what I thought the job would entail. I was also asked about any recent business issue that had caught my attention. Finally, I was asked to describe situations where I had demonstrated initiative and teamwork in the past. Although formal, the interview was relaxed and was a chance for me to get to know more about PwC.

At the end of the assessment day, we were invited to lunch with some current graduate trainees to wind down and ask any further questions that we had.

I was invited back to meet a director at the firm. He asked me a series of business-based questions which relied upon common sense rather than any prior business knowledge. For example, I remember one question being: 'You are a large supermarket chain in the north east and you are looking to open some new stores. What would you consider in making this decision?' He was looking for sensible suggestions and gave me plenty of time to think about my answers.

To prepare for the application process, I attended some PwC events at university and researched their website so that I had a good idea of what they did and who they were.

My advice would be to play to your strengths and be yourself. The group exercise is an opportunity to show that you can come up with sensible ideas but also that you can listen well to others. When it comes to the interview stage, I never felt like they were trying to 'catch me out'. They want to see people with confidence and enthusiasm who have a well-rounded life outside academia, as ultimately they will be putting you in front of their clients from an early stage.

8

Support through training

It can seem a long and lonely road when you are poring over accountancy books and study materials, especially after a hard day's work. It takes a lot of self-discipline and intellectual rigour. It can help to have someone to talk to for both morale and practical support. You need to be seen to be putting in the effort as well, so requesting holidays early on, in busy periods, or when examinations are looming is a no-no, and do not skip any classes or mock examinations. You will need to put in the necessary study hours and revision by planning your study timetable and sticking to it. Do not let friends and family talk you into partying when you should have your nose to the grindstone! You need to be sensible and take your training and career seriously.

With the larger firms, there are likely to be other trainees in the same boat as you. They will be there to compare notes with and provide mutual support. In smaller set-ups and internal roles, you could be the only one going through it at that particular time. Who will you turn to for support?

Your employing company

On official training schemes the company is expected, and perhaps contracted, to provide you with study leave, support with fees, and relevant and varied experience at the right time. Larger firms may have hundreds of trainees at the same time so they are well set up to give you training, development and coaching sessions and structured support, and they are committed to ensuring that you realise your true potential and achieve your goals. The selection, training and development of staff is costly, so they want to minimise failure and attrition for both the individual's and the company's sake.

Whether Public Practice or a company, employers will start with capable people who have strong problem-solving ability and commercial focus. They will value integrity and the talent to work well in a team and to build positive working relationships. They will appreciate the ability to learn from experience and even mistakes, and the ability to bring out the best in others, but they will also aim to build on such innate potential and softer people skills, through nurturing talent and ensuring that trainees acquire solid technical skills and develop both personally and professionally.

KPMG plans to take on in excess of 1,000 graduates, school leavers and interns in 2012, and claims to be the only firm with a dedicated full-time professional qualification training (PQT) team. The pass rates speak for themselves!

- They spread training over the three years, so that you will not be studying continuously. By the final and most technical papers, you will have two and a half years' practical experience to boost your understanding and maximise your chances of passing first time.

- They vary the type of training to include classroom and practical elements as well as online packages. This means you are able to progress at a pace to suit yourself.

- KPMG allows you to defer examinations if you feel insufficiently prepared. They do not place trainees under unnecessary stress and lower their confidence through failures.

- They have a strong diversity team to ensure that the necessary support is provided in cases of disability, illness, religious observance, and so on.

Nestlé is another company that helps its CIMA trainees by offering graduates financial support and generous study leave, which can be up to five days per examination.

Your boss

Obviously, your boss was once a trainee and, while no doubt busy themselves, they should be willing to help, advise and support you. Don't be too proud to admit that you are finding something difficult or to ask for an explanation of a topic. Not everyone is able to pass first time, but you don't want to be one of the people who fails. Pick your time carefully and request a quiet meeting – it is better to own up than completely mess up! Make sure you don't ask to meet when you are up against the clock or with imminent study or work deadlines. In any event, you should be having regular sessions with your direct line manager for setting targets and giving feedback on performance and progress. Ask to be given relevant, stretching and varied hands-on experience to help consolidate your learning.

Your personal career coach

Many firms will assign you a personal development mentor or coach who is committed to your career development. This is instead of your line manager, who can be more interested in your standard of work and therefore have conflicting objectives. The coach advises and supports you as you progress through the qualification and the organisation. Sometimes, you will also be allocated a peer 'buddy' for the induction stage.

Course tutors with training organisations

It harms training providers' reputations should you fail to pass your examinations, as they often market themselves on their students' success rates. This means that they should be happy to help and advise if you feel that you do not understand and are struggling with a certain paper or topic. They will usually allot a personal tutor, and they also run strategically timed revision programmes.

Professional bodies' student support services

The professional bodies will vary in what they offer you in terms of support throughout your training. Below, we've given you a few examples of the kind of support on offer. It's a really good idea to do some research into this and make the most of the resources available to you.

ICAEW/ACA

The list below from the ICAEW website identifies the ways in which professional bodies might support and advise you.

The ICAEW has a full-time, dedicated student support team to assist with:

- initial registrations

- Training Contract matters

- IPD and work-based learning

- friendly reminders of key dates and exam entry deadlines

- access to its award-winning business library and information service

- access to your local student network group via the student district societies

- examination-related enquiries

- change of address

- requests for literature

- overseas enquiries

- student discounts and offers

- up-to-date practice case studies

- and more.

Source: www.Icaew.com; studentsupport@icaew.com

CIMA

CIMA has a discussion forum and blog for students to network and post their queries; it is called CIMAsphere. It also produces a starter pack providing full information on the services CIMA offers. There is a dedicated students' area on its website and it publishes both student and professional member magazines. Go to www.cimaglobal.com/Employers/CIMA-Training/Student-support to find out more.

ACCA

ACCA emphasises its global reach for tuition, examination, employment and support:

- 83 offices and centres worldwide offering you support while you study

- 646 tuition providers worldwide

- over 380 exam centres in 170 countries so you can sit your exams locally

- 8,424 approved employers offering you quality study and training support.

Furthermore, the firm organises events, careers fairs and webinars where you can network or quiz examiners, as well as:

- webcasts

- exam technique events

- discussions on key topics affecting the profession.

See the website www.accaglobal.com/en/qualifications/why-acca/support.html for further details.

CIPFA

If you have queries and problems while working through the open learning materials, CIPFA runs a student helpline providing support on:

- exemptions

- examination and case study preparation

- examination deadlines and registration

- help with the Study Lounge

- the Initial Professional Development Scheme (IPDS).

You can email studentsupport@cipfa.org for more information.

Financial support

For ACA training, and when you are employed on a Training Contract, the employer will generally fund the cost of your first attempt at the training and examinations. Some training bodies will offer reductions for people paying their own fees. Obviously, you would be working and earning, but there may be opportunities for help with costs from grant-providing bodies, or through career development loans. See both www.turn2us.org.uk and www.direct.gov.uk/en/EducationAndLearning/AdultLearning/FinancialHelpForAdultLearners/CareerDevelopmentLoans.

As a registered student you will be eligible for an NUS student discount card, which can provide savings on travel, leisure, driving lessons and consumer products. Publishers will often offer reductions on books and even the *Financial Times*. See www.nus.org.uk/en/NUS-Extra/Discounts.

Relationships

If you are busy with work and study, your relationships could suffer as others might not get the attention they need or desire. You may be feeling sorry for yourself, but others may be feeling neglected and pushed out, too.

Don't let it be 'all work and no play'. It is important to create some balance in your life and to make sure that you have fun. You need to rest, recuperate and laugh for your physical and mental well-being.

Speak to your partner or a family member if you are irritable or stressed, explain how you are feeling and apologise for your tiredness or poor humour. Not only may they be pacified, but you may feel unburdened as well. Ask them to lighten the load by helping with more domestic chores when you are revising, and by allowing you space to think and study. Perhaps you could even get them involved and invite them to test you.

Counsellors

Examinations can be stressful, especially when your whole career seems to hinge on the outcome. Fear of failure can be cumulative, as you have to constantly live up to previous achievements. Instead of looking at the evidence and thinking 'Well, I did well before, why shouldn't I do well again?', people can start to feel like it was a fluke that they were successful before. They may feel that previous success was only because they worked so hard, but they won't be able to do it again.

If you start thinking negatively, then strategies for avoiding study might begin to emerge along with procrastination and obsessing. This needs to be nipped in the bud, and some cognitive behaviour therapy with a counsellor can give you valuable coping techniques and enable you to adjust how you talk to yourself and behave. Many larger firms provide private health insurance and employee benefit allowances that could fund this.

Try to remember that you have already been designated bright enough through the psychometric assessments during selection – so you clearly do have the ability. And if the other 424,000 qualified accountants in the world could pass their examinations, so can you!

9

Qualified: what next?

Post-qualification

Once qualified in accountancy, the career opportunities really open up. One of the joys of accountancy is that there are endless career possibilities, depending on how your interests, personality, skills and experience develop. You can move to different companies, roles, sectors and practice specialisms. As the common career paths figure in Chapter 3 showed, there is a great deal of potential movement, both upwards and sideways.

During the first few years, you will progress and develop through gaining experience and taking on greater responsibility. You may start supervising and leading others, working on more technically complex issues, or on higher-visibility, bigger-value projects for more important clients.

Public Practice

- In Public Practice, the structure tends to be quite formal. You will become increasingly responsible for managing risk and bringing in the business, and relationship-building is an increasingly important element of more senior roles. You will manage client relationships and identify opportunities for growing and developing the practice. You will also lead people initiatives.

- In audit, you would develop broad business knowledge and increasing technical competence in accounting, tax, accounting and IT processes, financial reporting and so on.

- In tax, you would take responsibility for more complex projects, maintaining quality while adhering to compliance standards.

- Advisory services include risk, mergers and acquisitions, corporate finance, business and financial management, and performance improvement offerings. You would be managing multiple projects of increasing complexity.

Post-qualification, you are no longer tied to your employer and you may decide to move to a larger or smaller practice where there are different types of challenges and opportunities. Widening your experience can be seen as an advantage as you will be building up your knowledge and skill set.

On completing your qualification you could expect to be in a senior role within two to three years, working through senior management and reaching executive director within nine to 12 years and achieving senior executive partner in 10 to 15 years.

Secondments

Once you become qualified in Public Practice, you might transfer to a different professional specialism such as tax, consultancy, forensic accountancy, risk, insolvency or corporate finance. Be aware that movement from tax in the opposite direction can be more difficult, because you may be viewed as too specialised, especially if you have studied tax rather than accountancy qualifications. Transfer between practice specialisms is easier at junior level, again before you are seen as too specialised.

Secondments can be varied; you might be seconded to an internal role on a client's site, or perhaps abroad to a different office. There are advantages of secondments as they can be a good way not only of gaining experience but also of trying out different fields without being committed. Most people planning a secondment or an external move do so within three years of qualification.

Of course, secondments abroad can sometimes be surprisingly difficult and not the 'jolly in the sun' you expect! You are there to do a job and it has been said that a surprising number of accountants seconded to offices abroad ask to return home early. The culture can be very different – it might be very serious and 'eyes down, no talking', which can be quite unlike the more relaxed and friendly London ethos. Weigh up the pros and cons and determine whether the secondment will benefit your career.

Mobility and working overseas

Equally, secondments are an option if you are working internally for a global firm. ACCA- and CIMA-qualified accountants may also relocate both in the UK and abroad, within or between companies, on a permanent or temporary basis.

When planning your career and selecting firms to apply to, it is obviously sensible to factor travel into the equation. You could ask about the opportunities to travel at interview. You cannot just assume that moving abroad will be an option, so if you are particularly interested in international experience you will want to base your decisions on this information. In all fields of accountancy, if you are prepared to be mobile and to relocate within and between firms, your promotion prospects and career progression will be aided.

Internal moves

When moving from Public Practice into an in-house role as an ACA-qualified accountant, your typical first position could be as an internal auditor, financial accountant, or perhaps a role in governance or business analysis, which is a quite objective and technical role. On the other hand, CIMA-qualified accountants have a broader commercial training and could move in a number of ways, such as:

- more senior financial roles

- into different sectors, such as banking, venture capital, manufacturing, retail, FMCG or perhaps the public sector

- into different functions, perhaps supply chain, marketing or strategy fields

- different careers, for instance management consultancy.

Similarly, the wide business and financial syllabus and strategic emphasis of ACCA mean that if you are ACCA-qualified you can also move into broader business management and consultancy.

With a CIPFA qualification, you might move in the opposite direction, from the public sector into Public Practice. However, if you stay in the public sector you might move upwards internally or to different governmental or not-for-profit concerns. Mobility can be vital for progression. Career paths in financial management tend to be structured but there are still opportunities to develop and specialise. Challenging and rewarding opportunities may be found in the NHS and local and central government, and within several years after qualification you may be taking responsibility for considerable resources or entire departments.

Most firms have qualified accountants in senior roles, whether as financial or operational directors or as CEOs. Some 20% of CEOs in FTSE 100 companies are qualified accountants.

Self-employment

There is always the option of starting your own accountancy practice with the relevant practising certificate. As an accountant, you will of course have a very good understanding of how to make a business successful and the internal controls required to cope with cashflow issues in the early days.

Management consultancy

Management consultancy is another future career move that you might consider; this could mean starting your own consultancy in the longer term or joining an established organisation. The Big Four audit firms have their own consulting divisions which provide services to manage talent, reduce costs and risk, improve quality, customer service, efficiency and performance, ensure smooth transactions in mergers and acquisitions, and advise on strategic direction. As a qualified accountant you could have a lot to contribute due to your technical, financial and business knowledge and experience. While it is possible to start as a new graduate, it is also common for experienced professionals to transfer to the consultancy division of their firm, or to a competitor, or into a smaller consultancy.

Continuing professional development (CPD)

Professional bodies and employers will recognise that qualification is the beginning, not the end, for professional development, and you would be required to keep up to date and professionally competent throughout your career.

ACA

IPD (initial professional development) is part of the ACA qualifying process and is required to integrate experience with academic studies and learned skills, through considering and recording issues relating to:

- business awareness

- ethics and professionalism

- personal effectiveness

- professional judgement

- technical and functional expertise.

Beyond qualification, CPD ensures ongoing currency and competence and maintains the reputation, credibility and value of your ACA accreditation. This may include building on communication and management skills, ethical awareness, business awareness and legal and regulatory knowledge. The ICAEW encourages you to 'reflect, act, impact and declare' and to:

- identify gaps in your knowledge, skills and competencies, perhaps as a result of changes in your environment, role, responsibilities or the world

- consider risks inherent in your role and the expectations others have of you, including your personal and technical weaknesses

- undertake appropriate learning and development activities to help you address these needs

- assess the effectiveness of these activities and consider whether your learning and development objectives have been met.

There is a great deal of freedom and flexibility in undertaking CPD. Development may be self-directed and via any medium to suit your lifestyle and personal needs. There is no set number of hours or points to attain; you just need to complete development when you feel it is required. You might attend courses, conferences, workshops or seminars, take additional electronic or classroom-based courses, or undertake personal reading, perhaps of professional magazines and technical journals. The only requirement is that you keep an online CPD record so that you can produce evidence of your continuing development should it ever be requested.

CIMA

Due to globalisation, CIMA recognises that financial management functions and regulations undergo constant change. In line with the International Federation of Accountants (IFAC) standard practice, CPD is required, but it is flexible and is considered your own responsibility. You will need to identify and address your needs for both professional and career development. A strong ethical code and integrity are not enough on their own; you need hard skills in areas such as project management, communication and teamwork as well.

CIMA's scheme emphasises the output rather than the number of hours or units of formal learning. The organisation feels that this best addresses its busy members' diverse working environments. You will be invited to regular training workshops and networking events. CIMA recognises over 100 employers as accredited partners providing relevant CPD and has developed a range of supporting CPD resources, valued planning tools and materials. Members are reported as saying that CPD activities have yielded positive results and do indeed further their careers. With three years' strategic experience, you can apply for CIMA Fellowship (FCMA), which adds further weight to a CV.

Each year CIMA selects a sample of its members to monitor their CPD, so it is important to keep on top of this.

CIPFA

CPD is mandatory for CIPFA members too, with many public-sector bodies operating accredited staff development programmes. Career progression requires learning through meetings, conferences and training courses.

The CIPFA Learning Centre enables members to manage their CPD online and access authoritative learning materials. Your minimum requirement is 20 hours in one year and 120 hours over three years. CPD does not have to be through a paid-for course: it is anything that enhances your skills and knowledge relevant to the job, even volunteering your services to a community group or a CIPFA panel or working group. By recording and planning your CPD, you should be better able to identify areas of expertise or development needs for career progression.

ACCA

ACCA emphasises that professionalism is about lifelong learning in order to meet the needs of a changing market. Again, you are afforded flexibility and control over how much and what development activities you choose to undertake, but if you are an active member of ACCA you will have to complete CPD on an annual basis. ACCA has introduced Realise, a professional development programme to help plan, manage and record progress in building learning and skills, alongside codes of ethics and professionalism. This scheme provides clear reassurance that you are keeping yourself up to date.

ACCA recognises certain approved employers that provide excellent development and training, and lists accredited CPD training providers of face-to-face courses, technical updates, qualifications and presentations. The organisation also provides a virtual learning centre with a wide range of courses and materials for Public Practice.

The future of accountancy

Moving with the times

As new blood enters the accounting profession, we are seeing more online accounting systems being established, with reports of online accounting vendors being mobbed for demonstrations at conferences! Moving with the times, the power of social media is also being embraced by some in the accounting world, as Twitter and LinkedIn become the preferred channels to generate business and engage with clients.

Sustainability and ethics

CSR is increasingly recognised as important in today's world, both to attract clients, investors and potential employees, and to maintain a positive, ethical, honourable and altruistic image with stakeholders and the wider community.

Professional bodies and accountancy firms want to be seen as 'giving something back', and therefore they are concerned not only about integrity relating to legal and governance issues, but also about people and environmental concerns, for example reducing their carbon footprint. Accountancy professionals clearly need to be just as vigilant and enlightened in advising clients as they are in working for their own employers. The stereotypical, 'black or white' accountant would more naturally concentrate on the bottom line, and perhaps neglect to invest in more nebulous image factors or to incorporate CSR initiatives into strategy. Sweatshops may reduce costs but they will be bad for business – fair trade and 'environmentally friendly' sells! Sponsorship and donation of funds raise a company's profile and image. Good pay, perks, and training and development attract and keep quality employees, so sustainability can be seen as important not just ethically but also commercially.

Around 85% of FTSE company boards include at least one ICAEW member, so accountants are ideally placed to influence on a firm's ethical performance in addition to its commercial efficiency. Ethical components are increasingly included, and indeed weighted heavily, in accountancy training and professional development.

- CIMA and the Department for Environment, Food and Rural Affairs (DEFRA) have actively collaborated to design a climate resilience toolkit.

- ICAEW has launched an e-learning business sustainability programme.

- Ethics, social and environmental issues are at the heart of the ACCA qualification. One compulsory business analysis paper requires students to examine the impact of social and environmental factors on the strategy of a business, and the scope of CSR in relation to the expectations of stakeholders.

The Prince of Wales is keen for sustainability in accountancy to become part of the DNA of businesses today and tomorrow. The Accounting for Sustainability project (www.accountingforsustainability.org) is working with multidisciplinary agencies, including public, not-for-profit and commercial organisations, professional bodies, investors and academics, to develop key guidelines and tools to ensure that sustainability is fundamental to reporting and decision-making.

Globalisation

Accountancy bodies listen to their members and tailor learning and support to address their members' needs. At the same time as incorporating sustainability and ethics into their curricula, they are also considering globalisation. Growing globalisation is increasingly not just about career mobility, but also about the need for standardised international practices and a greater concern and focus on sustainability factors. Over the next couple of years, the UK GAAP accounting standards will become merged with, or may be superseded by, International Financial Reporting Standards (IFRS). As the global downturn demonstrated, we are all inextricably linked and intertwined.

Globalisation has also increased competition and has led to greater outsourcing of business processes and shared services. Outsourced functions may not only be in a different part of the country, but even in a different part of the world! Cheaper and more advanced telecommunications are having an ever-increasing impact on businesses. Accountants need to recognise and run with such changes. Of course, technological advances may also free up finance professionals from more mundane and routine accounting and give them more time for involvement in strategic and commercial decision-making.

Conclusion

Accountancy has always been a sought-after qualification and a ticket to a successful career, whether in professional practice or as a springboard into a senior commercial or managerial role. The profession's future is rosy, and now is a great time to start your career in accountancy.

In this competitive market, qualifications count. Employers demand ever-higher grades, more prestigious qualifications, and directly relevant experience. However, firms are also introducing school-leaver schemes to attract strong candidates earlier, and with the raising of university fees it may be that fewer people go for graduate entry and greater numbers select school-leaver and the AAT or CAT routes instead.

There is said to be a global shortage of finance qualified professionals, and companies are increasingly turning to accountants to help them weather the current economic storm. Those prepared to take a tough stance on risk, costs and waste, including changes to executive rewards and bonus schemes, are being welcomed.

A high demand for qualified accountants is being predicted, often for opposing reasons. When times are bad, accountants are needed to manage the negative situation. When things are improving, more accountants will be needed to meet the demand due to the economic growth and to manage the increasingly complex accounting and reporting procedures. Whichever is the case, sound judgement and communication will be required, with fluency in current affairs to complement technical excellence. The bottom line is that accountancy will remain the universal language of business.

There are so many routes into accountancy that there will be one to suit each different personality and situation. We hope that in this book you've found the information and tools you need to decide what's right for you, and to take your first steps into your long and successful accounting career.

Useful resources

Professional accountancy bodies

- **Institute of Chartered Accountants in England and Wales (ICAEW):** www.icaew.com

- **Institute of Chartered Accountants of Scotland:** www.icas.org.uk

- **Institute of Chartered Accountants in Ireland:** www.charteredaccountants.ie

- **Association of Chartered Certified Accountants (ACCA):** www.accaglobal.com

- **Chartered Institute of Management Accountants (CIMA):** www.cimaglobal.com

- **Chartered Institute of Public Finance and Accountancy (CIPFA):** www.cipfa.org.uk

- **National Audit Office:** www.nao.org.uk

- **NHS Graduate Management Scheme:** www.nhsgraduates.co.uk

- **London Treasurers' Graduate Finance Scheme (local government):** www.financethefuture.com

- **Institute of Financial Accountants (IFA):** www.ifa.org.uk

- **Chartered Institute of Taxation (CIOT):** www.tax.org.uk

- **Association of International Accountants (AIA):** www.aiaworldwide.com

- **Association of Corporate Treasurers (ACT):** www.treasurers.org

- **Association of Accounting Technicians (AAT):** www.aat.org.uk

Accountancy qualifications

A list of accredited training providers for each professional body may be found on the tuition provider pages of the professional bodies' websites and also at www.accountancystudents.co.uk/directory (click on 'Tuition Providers').

Financial support

- **Turn2us (financial support):** www.turn2us.org.uk

- **Professional and Career Development Loans:** www.direct.gov.uk/en/EducationAndLearning/AdultLearning/FinancialHelpForAdultLearners/CareerDevelopmentLoans

- **National Union of Students:** www.nus.org.uk/en/NUS-Extra/Discounts

Support for school leavers

- **Kaplan Financial:** http://financial.kaplan.co.uk and http://kaplanapprenticeships.co.uk

- **The Apprenticeship Scheme:** www.apprenticeships.org.uk

- **Funding in Scotland, Skills Development Scotland:** www.skillsdevelopmentscotland.co.uk

- **Funding in Wales, Welsh Government:** www.new.wales.gov.uk

- **Funding in Northern Ireland, Department for Employment and Learning:** www.delni.gov.uk

Vacancy information

Internships

- www.internoptions.com

- http://targetjobs.co.uk

- www.allaboutcareers.com

- www.milkround.com

- www.ratemyplacement.co.uk

Trainee vacancies may be found on the websites of the professional bodies. See also:

- **Accountancy Age Jobs:** www.accountancyagejobs.com

- **Accountant Careers:** www.accountantcareers.co.uk

- **Association of Chartered Certified Accountants:** www.accaglobal.com

- **Randstad:** www.randstadfp.com

- **Careers in Audit:** www.careersinaudit.com

- **Local Government Jobs:** www.lgjobs.com

- **SWAT UK:** www.swat.co.uk

Interview preparation

- **Psychometric tests:** www.jobtestprep.co.uk

- **Assessment Day:** www.assessmentday.co.uk

General accountancy information

- **Accounting Web:** www.accountingweb.co.uk

- **Public Finance:** www.publicfinance.co.uk

- **PQ magazine:** www.pqaccountant.com

Accounting and the environment

- **Accounting for Sustainability project:** www.accountingforsustainability.org

General careers information

- **Accountancy Students:** www.accountancystudents.co.uk

- **AllAboutCareers:** www.allaboutcareers.com

- **Prospects:** www.prospects.ac.uk

- **Inside Careers:** www.insidecareers.co.uk

- **UCAS:** www.ucas.com

Index of advertisers